Published by
The Junction
8-14 Bishop Street
Derry Londonderry
BT48 6PW

ISBN: 978-0-9935037-1 9

This publication has received support from the Department of Foreign Affairs and Trade, Dublin, through its Reconciliation/Anti-Sectarian Funds. The views expressed do not necessarily reflect those of the Department.

REFORMED ALWAYS TO BE REFORMED
THE REFORMATIONS THEN AND NOW

Introduction

This short publication is about a long lasting revolution in modern European history. If you want to read a more substantial publication, all 757 pages, then engage with the 2016 publication by Carlos M. N. Eire, *Reformations: The Early Modern World, 1450-1650*. It will take you longer and it is a work of remarkable depth and scope. This is much shorter but hopefully offers a helpful overview with some contemporary challenges.

What happened in the sixteenth century changed Europe and the legacies endure. The plural *'Reformations'* is used, because there was not one Reformation, but many. Protestantism took many different forms, each with their differences, bringing about denominationalism, which has continued to fragment to the present. There was also an influential Catholic Reformation and it is important to recognise the symbiosis between the Protestant Reformations and the Catholic Reformation. At every point they were interrelated. During the sixteenth century Europe divided into a Protestant North and a Catholic South. The most bitter wars in Christian history were fought at this time. The religious map of Europe took shape. Ireland experienced the Reformations, Anglican, Reformed and Catholic, producing a bitter, sectarianised and violent history. Ireland is largely free from violence now but not altogether from sectarianism, especially in Northern Ireland.

The Reformations were more than religious. They were also political, economic and cultural. It is important, therefore, to understand the sixteenth century Reformations in context and in their complexity, and to grasp the connections between religion, moral and ethical dynamics, social, political, economic and cultural life. We are realizing again that these are not now as separate and religion is not as private as a recent phase in our Western thought has made out. Life is more complex and indivisible than we have imagined.

In twelve short chapters there is an explanation of the dynamics and forces that led to the Reformations. There is also a critical examination of religion and political violence, women and the Reformations, and the radical legacies of the Protestant Principle and reformed always to be reformed. We no longer live in the sixteenth century and our twenty-first century questions are different. In a declining West we are now faced with challenges to reform our political, economic and cultural systems and institutions. How can theology respond to a crisis of Western legitimacy and what shape does a public and interreligious theology and ethical praxis take? For Christian faith communities in relation to other globalised religions, what will *'reformed'* theology and ethics look like? These are our contemporary challenges.

My thanks to Richie Hetherington for his word-processing skills and gift to be able to decipher my unreformed handwriting! My thanks also to Maureen Hetherington for handling all the publication logistics and her commitment to the programme, and to Gerard Deane, Holywell Trust, for supporting the programme.

Johnston McMaster
Advent 2016

1
Europe of the Sixteenth Century

Everything happens in a context and is shaped by that context. The Reformations of the sixteenth century were revolutionary in the changes they introduced, not only to religious life, but to political, cultural and economic life. Life in the sixteenth century was such that there were no twenty-first century divisions between religion, politics, culture and economics. The religious-secular divide came centuries later. Sixteenth century Europe was Christendom and Christendom was Europe and religion and politics were inseparable. The Reformations took place in the sixteenth century and not all of the issues and questions can be projected onto the twenty-first century. Not all of the questions and answers of the time are ours. We cannot therefore draw a neat set of correspondences, still less treat the Reformations in 2017, the 500th anniversary, as contemporary struggles, battles and questions still to be engaged. Context, then and now makes that impossible. It is important, therefore, to look critically and carefully at the Europe of the sixteenth century.

When Martin Luther on the 31 October 1517 nailed his ninety-five theses to the Church door in Wittenberg, he had no breakfast that morning. He had no breakfast any morning! Most Europeans didn't do breakfast in the 1500s. The day consisted of two meals, dinner at 11.00 am and supper at 5.00 pm. Movement into towns began to change the two-meal rhythm. Longer working hours made supper later and the main meal became a later dinner. So something was needed before lunchtime, and as boys went to school for long lessons, workers and boys needed breakfast. By 1600 there was a new routine. You washed your hands and face, cleaned your teeth, had breakfast and went to work or school by 8.00 am.[1] In the 1500s Luther had no breakfast.

Dates and times were another matter of what now seems confusing cultural difference. Today we would say that the sixteenth century began on 1 January 1501. In Flanders it was Easter Day, in Russia on 1 September and in the German states, for Luther, New Year began on 25 December. It was the difference between the Julian and Gregorian calendars, the latter introduced in 1582. Even religion divided time with Protestant countries holding on to the old Roman Julian calendar into the eighteenth century rather than the one introduced by Pope Gregory in 1582. New Years day then in London and Florence was on 25 March but 25 March came ten days earlier for Florentines![2] Many more cultural changes were introduced in the sixteenth century, which means that the world of the Reformations and our world are planets apart. There were other social and cultural changes with massive implications.

The fourteenth century was one of agrarian crises, famine and the great plague. Population growth in Europe had outgrown food supply and famine was widespread. This left the population weak and malnourished. There were outbreaks of typhoid and eventually the Black Death, which took several forms, bubonic, pneumonic and septicaemia plague. It originated in the Far East and was carried on board ships by rats carrying plague-ridden fleas. Densely populated and filthy cities bred rats with the deadly fleas. Some 30% of Europe's population died in the Black Plague. It was so bad and so contagious that family and friends deserted the sick and left them in agony to die alone. In the sixteenth century elements of the plague were still around and in 1527 it struck Luther's part of Germany.

Life in the words of English philosopher, Thomas Hobbes, was *"nasty, brutish and short"*. The Black Plague was traumatic. It was seen as God's punishment. Some saw it as a Jewish plot. Death and the fear of death were real. Life was short. People were preoccupied with dying, heaven, hell and purgatory. From 1337-1453 there was the Hundred Years War between France and England. It produced Joan of Arc. There were growing tensions between peasants and lords or landowners. A decreasing peasant population made it more expensive to hire labourers. With fewer to feed prices dropped. The holdings of noble and clerical landowners were at serious economic risk, and these landowners included many ecclesiastical Lords.[3] All of this was the context in which the Reformations happened.

There was a global context. The century that preceded the Reformations was the century of discovery. The larger world was discovered, that is from a European perspective. Just as those photographs of planet earth taken from spacecraft have changed our self-perception, our awareness of who we are in the cosmos, so the European navigators between 1492 and 1500 *'discovered'* two new continents, North and South America. Immediately afterwards they *'discovered'* the southern half of Africa. Now Europe had discovered three continents full of fabulous wealth. Were these *'discoveries'* or conquests? This was the political and economic drive for European expansion. It was the beginning of the European empires and 500 years of European hegemony. The Spanish and the Portuguese were building massive and very wealthy empires. Christianity was part of the imperial expansionism. Missionaries also journeyed with the explorers or conquerors. Political, economic and religious imperialism were inseparable. Within two decades of European expansionism to the Americas and Africa, the Reformations were under way.

A revolution that was even greater than that of the Reformations, and without which there might not have been Reformations, was the invention of the printing press. The media revolution changed everything. Once communication became widespread, so too did education. Europe discovered paper from the Chinese. Marco Polo brought inexpensive linen rag paper from China and then good ink was developed. The next step followed with the invention of moveable, metal type in mid-fifteenth century Rhineland. This has been described as *"the single most important invention of the last one thousand years"*.[4] By 1455, Johannes Gutenberg had printed the Bible in Latin at Mainz. For the next fifty years books were expensive and even if some could afford them, many probably could not read them. Yet the printing revolution was to spark the education revolution and, significant as Gutenberg's invention of print was, it was others who in the sixteenth century put his invention to wider and more radical use.

The earliest printing experts came from Germany and through the developed technology of printing new ideas spread like wildfire. Luther created a book market and in his city of Wittenberg there were seven shops given solely to the printing of writings by Luther and his colleagues. Texts and pamphlets were printed in the thousands. *"By Luther's death in 1546 over 3,400 editions of the Bible in whole or part had appeared in High German and about 430 editions in Low German".*[5] In total this means about a million copies of the Bible in print. But it was not just typeface print. The Reformations propaganda was visual and included pictures, images and cartoons. "The dominant publicist was Martin Luther".[6]

The printing revolution of the fifteenth century may be an even greater revolution than the IT revolution of our time. It put the message out there, was a propagandist revolution and at the same time an educational revolution. Printing changed the world and made the Reformations possible.

The world that led to the Reformations and in which the Reformations happened was a world of major change and upheaval. In such a context of change, of cultural shifts, deadly plague and the living reality of death, European expansionism with political power and greater wealth for a few, peasant revolts and decades long war, the print revolution and explosion of new ideas and knowledge, all of this meant radical upheaval and change in how people saw things, perceived the world and themselves. It led to identity crises and a crisis of values. *"The major crisis of the late medieval period was a crisis of values".*[7] At the heart of the crisis *"was the tottering of the symbols of security".*[8] It is when symbols of meaning which provide people with a sense of security, begin to fall that there is a deep existential crisis, a collapse of the sense of who we are, of meaning and purpose. There is a psychological trauma. In the medieval world the basis and guarantor of security was the church. The radically changing world was testing values and beliefs. Change always does, and the powerful

Christendom church did not exist outside of this context of radical change and upheaval. It too would have to change, which meant change in its power and authority, including its dominant political role. What the upheaval and change did for the Church was to create a major existential crisis, which totally undermined and shattered the church as symbol and guarantor of security. The western schism and the strong anti-clericalism destroyed the medieval world's most powerful symbol of meaning and security. The Reformations were the beginning of the end for Christendom. It would take another 400 years and a catastrophic European (global) war to end European imperialism and at the same time kill European imperial Christianity or Christendom. But the death throes began in the sixteenth century, and as 1911 1910 created a European crisis of values, so the 1500s called values into question. The old was shattering and no one knew quite what would replace it. The Western church was never the same again. Europe did not remain the same. *"…Luther's stance in 1517 led to the most dramatic religious upheaval of the last thousand years"*.[9] It was also a political, cultural and social upheaval. Luther may not have started the upheaval, but he shaped the revolution.

The world of the sixteenth century Reformations is not our world and many of its questions and issues are not our questions and issues. But we learn from it in a time when there is a crisis of legitimacy for the European Union, as Europe painfully comes to terms with its political and economic decline in the world and seeks to get over the loss of European hegemony. We too have a crisis of values, a different context, but one in which reform, at many levels, awaits a burst of new ideas.

2
Reformations Before
the Reformations

Reformations did not begin on the 31 October 1517 when Martin Luther nailed his 95 theses to the church door in Wittenberg. Reformation had been in the air for up to three centuries. There were numbers of people who saw the need for change and were even optimistic that it could happen. Where corruption becomes apparent the need for reform becomes imperative. And the idea of reform was an idea as old as Christianity itself. Reform movements go back a long way. Christianity in Ireland was a thousand years old when the Luther reform movement began and there already had been reform in the early Irish church. There has always been a gap between idealism and realism, between the highest intentions and the actual practice. In a sense the church always lives in the tension between human sinfulness and the ideas of Christian perfection. *"All have sinned and fallen short of the glory of God"* alongside the call of Jesus *"to be perfect as your Father in heaven is perfect"*. Even if the Lukan version is preferred to the Matthean, "be compassionate even as your Father in heaven is compassionate", there is a considerable gap between humans missing the mark and the practice of compassion. Perhaps this was the realism of the sixteenth century Reformation focus on *"semper reformanda"*, the church reformed always to be reformed. Reform is ongoing and continuous, not least because there is no perfectionism, but always flaws, weaknesses and even corruption.

The medieval world was not the world of the twenty-first century. In the West the secular is dominant and a huge gap has opened up between sacred and secular, faith and politics, and religion has become privatized. Religion in medieval Europe was an integral part of life, interwoven with pretty much every aspect of life and living. Religious reform, therefore, was also social, cultural and political reform and this is why the reform of the sixteenth century was such a revolutionary challenge. Luther not only sparked radical reform within the church, the reform created social, cultural and political upheaval.

Medieval Europe was a place of clerical corruption and much dissent. There were bishops who were absentees from their dioceses and those who held more than one office or appointment. Nepotism was rife with the appointment of relatives to high office. As well as keeping it in the family it was also possible to buy church offices. The authorities were on the make. Underlying all of this was the question of authority from the Pope down. Especially in the fifteenth century *the abuses and failings of the church became more conspicuous, more openly discussed, and more deeply resented by a wider spectrum of people*.[10]

Early reform had been called for by Francis of Assisi. Francis committed himself to a life of poverty and created a new order within the church with an emphasis on poverty and preaching. There was nothing new about the vow of poverty but it was a new expression of dissent in the face of growing church wealth and power. It was a denial of power and wealth, even though his radical poverty became problematic for his order.

Before Francis was an earlier influence for reforms. The Cathars or Albigensians belonged to the thirteenth century and believed that matter was the creation of an evil deity and that the church and Pope were corrupt. The reaction of the church was to seek to crush the Cathars through the crusade of 1209-1229 and the introduction of the Inquisition. There was also the emergence of the Waldensians' founded by a layperson, Peter Waldo. The Waldensians were characterized by radical poverty and public preaching. Even though milder in their approach than the Cathars, they were condemned as heretics by the Pope in 1184.

These two movements undoubtedly had an influence on Francis. He may not have been declared heretical, but Papal opposition did come through a series of papal bulls which declared the Franciscan position to be wrong and reaffirmed that private property was an inherent human right. It was all the more remarkable that Francis was canonized two years after his death in 1226. Authority, wealth, property and power were all at the heart of dissent and the clamor for reform.

In England John Wycliffe was a voice of dissent and for reform. He was an Oxford philosopher and in line with the Waldensians he produced two documents, *On Divine Lordship* (1375) and *On Civil Lordship* (1376). Core to Wycliffe's position was that Christ was the head of the Church, not the Pope (the authority question) and the Bible was the supreme guide in relation to doctrine, ritual and morals (authority again). A radical dimension to his thought was that all authority, whether civil or church, came from God and therefore relativized all human authority and *"All Lordship, then, was contingent on performance … This meant that anyone who failed to live up to the duties of his office should be removed from it, including the Pope"*.[11] Prosperity could also be removed from corrupt clerics. Not surprisingly Wycliffe was excommunicated in 1377 and removed from his teaching post. Several decades after he died in 1384, church authorities ordered his bones to be exhumed and burnt for heresy.

Wycliffe did start a movement of followers called by the nickname of Lollards, which meant *"mumblers who talked nonsense"*. They lost out eventually but not before translating the Vulgate Bible into English so that the ordinary people could read it and understand it for themselves. They agreed with Wycliffe as to the unchallengeable authority of the Bible.

In central Europe in the kingdom of Bohemia another, not unconnected reform movement began led by John Hus. Prague had a great cathedral and an equally great university. Hus, before becoming rector of the university, preached some very radical sermons, much like Wycliffe, attacking the church. Identity politics were also involved as Czech nobility were deeply resentful of the interference in their affairs by church authorities. This was about Czech identity against the German speakers in the Bohemian church. Hus, like the later Luther, was embroiled in contemporary politics and there was no great dividing line between faith and politics.

In 1414 Hus did something really provocative, when he and his followers began to offer consecrated wine as well as bread in their Eucharists. This was not the practice of the church and *"the Eucharistic chalice containing the wine was to become a cherished symbol of the 'Hussite' movement"*.[12] In 1415 Hus was betrayed by a Council of clerics, was imprisoned in terrible conditions, and burned at the stake. He became a Czech martyr, which in turn created such anger in Prague that a separate Bohemian church was established and the Eucharist became the symbol of a revolution. His death was *"a powerful symbol that the institutional Church was no longer capable of dealing constructively with a movement of reform"*.[13]

With various wars and conflicts it was easy to believe, as many did, that the Last Days were arriving. This was strong in Italy and someone who gave voice to such theological perspective was the Dominican Girolamo Savonarola. In the 1490s he was preaching about the Last Days and claiming visions and direct communication from the Almighty. There was political invisibility. Power was fading for the famous Medici family and in Florence Savonarola was thundering against all kinds of immorality and corruption. The monarchy was replaced by the first republic in history. Savonarola directly addressed princes, prelates and noblemen, calling them to penance before the sword was unsheathed. In 1495 he was excommunicated by the Pope from what he called the *'Babylon of Rome'* and in 1498 he, with supporters, was tortured and burned at the stake. Savonarola's prison writings were read by Archbishop Thomas Cranmer before he went to the stake in 1556. His memory was much treasured by an Italian devotional guild, which produced the spiritual classic, the *Imitation of Christ.*

The clamour for reform was not new by the beginning of the sixteenth century of the Reformations. It had been obvious for much of the previous three centuries. The medieval Church was aware of it. At the Fifth Lateran Council in 1512, an Augustinian and future cardinal, Egidio da Viterbo gave the opening address and warned the Pope that the Church needed to turn back to its old and ancient brilliance. He said, *"celestial and human beings … crave renewal"*.[14] Five years later in Germany the craving for renewal exploded into an inextinguishable fireball.

3
The Role of Humanism, Then and Now

There may well have been no sixteenth century Reformations without the Renaissance and humanism. The Renaissance was about the advent of new ideas and new learning. In one sense there was nothing new in the Renaissance. It was the recovery of the Greek classical civilization applied to the contemporary situation. The values and worldview of ancient Greece and Rome were being used to test and call into question the medieval world. Things were wrong, there was corruption and abuse of power, yet reform, rebirth or renewal was in the air. Authority, of which the Church had been the fount, was collapsing. Could it stand against the values and ideas of ancient Greece and Rome? Recovering the classical model the Renaissance did create a new paradigm, which was an evolutionary stage through the Reformations and Scientific Revolution to the Enlightenment. The latter still largely shapes our Western worldview, though a radical shift is taking place as we have moved into what is known as the post-modern.

If the core characteristic of the Renaissance was *'independence of mind'*, then the power and authority of the medieval Church was not going to survive. The Church had been dominant and theology was the dominant science, but change was under way. The Church began to move from the centre of society and found itself confined more and more to the religious sphere. Scientists, philosophers, artists, writers and the princes were all freed from the monopolistic and totalitarian Church. This was unprecedented freedom and it was a Church in the process of being defanged. The world did not need the Church to control and dictate and humanity could be human without the dictates of theology. Human beings could control their own destiny and improve their lot.

The new learning of the fifteenth century, according to Norman Davies, possessed three novel features:

- *The cultivation of long neglected classical authors, especially Cicero and Homer.*
- *The cultivation of ancient Greek as an essential partner to Latin.*
- *The rise of biblical scholarship based on a critical study of the original Hebrew and Greek texts.*[15]

The Renaissance was therefore the recovery of the ancient humanist tradition with its human values and ideas. The result was an expansion and development of humanist circles. These were found in Oxford, Salamanca and Cracow and the paradoxical thing was that the patrons of humanism were Church people, cardinals no less!

The roots of this rediscovered humanism lay in Italy. In 1485 an intact female body was unearthed in Rome. She was probably a contemporary of Jesus and Paul, but the real significance was that Rome had recovered its classical past. She had been dead for fifteen hundred years but she was preserved, her beauty there for all to see, her thick styled hair and pink lips, all offering to Roman citizens, pleasure and astonishment. The grandiose of ancient Rome had been brought back to life! Her body decomposed soon after but Rome had had a live encounter with the past. It was a Greco-Roman past and could that classical past live again?

> *Few slogans have captured the essence of an era so perfectly as 'Ad fontes!' or, 'Return to the sources'. These words were much more than a trendy slogan in the fifteenth and sixteenth century: they were also a battle cry, a paradigm for genuine reform.*[16]

Returning to sources meant getting back to the ancient Greeks and Romans and the early Christians. This was a privileged past that had to be recovered and one which could radically call into question the present structures of power and authority, and the corruption, abuses of power and value deficit.

Many now embraced the new paradigm, none more so than Erasmus of Rotterdam (1469-1536). He was the supreme humanist scholar, the son of a priest, who was expected to follow into the Church. He did enter an Augustinian monastery, hated it and fell in love with another monk. He left and became secretary to the Bishop of Cambrai. He was ordained priest in 1492 but shaped an independent career, *"the roving international man of letters who lived off the proceeds of his writings and money provided by admirers"*.[17] He frequently visited London and Cambridge and he became a popular writer. He imbibed the new humanist learning and then turned from the secular literature and applied the humanist learning to Christian texts. For Erasmus there was no dichotomy between humanism and Christian faith. He created a Christian humanism being a devoted humanist and a devoted Christian.

Two very influential books followed. *Folly's Praise of Folly* was published in 1511 and ran to forty-three editions. Earlier he had published *Handbook of a Christian Soldier* (1503). He learned Greek, which gave him access to the New Testament text and the writings of early Greek theologians. Critical editions of early Christian texts flowed from his pen and the great centrepiece of his work was the 1516 Greek New Testament. More than anything else this inspired future reformers. This work moved beyond the standard translation in Latin, the Vulgate. Erasmus was dealing critically with the original text or language. His bombshell translation was Mathew 3 v 2 where Jerome in the Vulgate had translated John the Baptist's cry as *'do penance'*. This had become the medieval Church's theological basis for the sacrament of penance. Erasmus translated the Greek, *metanoeite*, as *'come to your senses, turn around, repent'*. That was radically different and it was a translation that undermined a medieval theology of penance.

Furthermore, Erasmus attacked the dominant biblical interpretative approach of allegory. Scholars allegorised biblical texts, especially obscure ones. Allegory was the basis of an approach to Mary. Her perpetual virginity was based on an allegorical reading of Ezekiel 44 v 2. Erasmus did not totally deny allegory but urged caution and common sense. Now Erasmus had unearthed a troublesome problem. Did the Bible have all sacred truth or was tradition authoritative also? So *'ad fontes'*, *"return to the sources"*, became a major issue of the Reformations. It was the question of authority again.

Erasmus did not share Augustinian pessimism about human nature. He preferred another early theologian Origen whose anthropology was based on a Pauline text from the Letter to the Thessalonians. Humans are made up of flesh, spirit and soul. Flesh, Origen said, was corrupt but spirit was intact. Erasmus wrote much on the spirit in his theology. *"There was a spiritual basis for humanist optimism in the face of Augustine"*.[18]

The Preface to his Greek New Testament in 1516, the year before Luther nailed his theses to the church door, is almost poetic,

> *I wish that every woman might read the gospel and the Epistles of St Paul. Would that these were translated into every language … and understood not only by Scots and Irishmen but by Turks and Saracens. Would that the farmer might sing snatches of Scripture at his plough, that the weaver might hum phrases of Scripture to the time of his shuttle…*[19]

The humanist recovery that began with the unearthing of the intact young female body in Rome in 1485 shaped the Reformations. The intellectual movement took a human centred view of the world and shaped a whole new focus on the uniqueness and worth of the individual. That in time shaped the Protestant emphasis on the individual conscience and in art there was a renewed emphasis on the human body. There were political implications as well, as Christendom was challenged and replaced by the sovereign state and the early rise of nationalism. The Reformations when they came did not dismantle

Christendom, the Reformers bought into it, but Renaissance humanism started the Christendom rot. Core to Renaissance humanism was education. The new human world came about through education and education included the development of mental and physical talents in young people. So gymnastics was taught alongside Greek and Latin.[20] Christian teaching was not excluded but theology was no longer the queen of the sciences, no longer the controlling, master narrative. Yet for Erasmus and many more there was no contradiction between their humanism and their faith, though faith was being interpreted differently. Humanism was about the liberation of the human mind and will. Humanism was not just about looking back. It looked forward and it created new learning, new scholarship and new piety.

> *Humanism shattered the reigning paradigms that had guided Western Christendom for a millennium, inspiring a new confidence in the powers of the human intellect, promoting new kinds of inquiry, giving voice to a critique of the past and the status quo that was at once radical and utterly conservative. Something of that magnitude cannot happen overnight.*[21]

Without humanism there would have been no Reformations. If Scripture was a central plank of the Reformations then without the critical study of Scripture introduced by the humanists, reformers would not have dreamt of the lost virtues of a primitive and early Christianity. We might improve the metaphor but the point is made. *"Erasmus laid the egg and Luther hatched it".*[22]

4
The Classical Protestant Reformations

As the fifteenth century drew to a close, many Europeans believed they were in the last days. Orthodox Christians and Muslims were convinced that in 1492-1493, the end of the world would come. Like all such dates proposed in history for the End, it came and went and the world carried on. But 1500 was considered a momentous date as a millennium and a half had passed since the birth of Christ. These were momentous times and with a craving for reform of the Church in the air, it was a time of expectation. It was also an insecure time. In eastern and southern Europe the Muslim Ottoman empire was on the move, taking the Balkans. The Ottoman empire would threaten the very gates of Vienna, but further west in 1492, the Muslim kingdom of Granada was recovered by a Spanish kingdom. Expectation and upheaval were the existing context for Martin Luther's public career.

The Lutheran Reformation

Luther arrived in the new university of Wittenberg as a lecturer in 1511. He came as an already troubled person. In 1505 he was caught up in a terrible thunderstorm, was terrified and prayed to St Anne, the mother of Mary, that if he survived he would enter monastic life. He joined the Augustinians and it was his House that sent him to Wittenberg. Augustine's pessimistic theology of the sinful human had influenced Luther. He had been taught it for nine years, but there was also a humanist influence and it was this humanist influence that encouraged him to question the dominant scholastic approach to theology. Two years after his arrival Luther began to lecture on the Psalms, providing his students with texts of the Psalms without the customary commentary, but with wide margins for students' own reflections. He was encouraging his students to take a fresh and perhaps original look at the Psalms. In 1515 he began lectures on Paul's Letter to the Romans and this meant dealing with the text that influenced Augustine so much. It was in his lectures on Romans that Luther discovered for himself good news.

After the *Fall* in Genesis, humans are trapped without escape in sin and are *"turned in on themselves"*. And then he hit on Romans 1 v 17, a quotation from Habbakuk 2 v 4, *"he who through faith is righteous shall live"*. Since righteousness and righteous were translated in Jerome's Vulgate as *justitia/justus*, Luther constructed his core theology of justification by faith. Luther's reading of Romans also set law over against grace and the Psalms were reflections on the significance of Jesus. All of this painted Judaism as a legalistic, negative religion, put Jesus in opposition to his own Jewish roots and was heavily supersessionist, Christianity had superseded Judaism and was superior. The radical and social significance of justice in the Hebrew Bible, underpinning the Romans text was missed. Yet justification by faith became the central watchword of the Protestant Reformations and undoubtedly was good news and liberating for Luther and many in the sixteenth century. It also became the core of Lutheranism and key to the Lutheran model of the Reformations. It took over four hundred years for a Lutheran bishop to critically suggest that Luther may have misread Romans and the Hebrew Bible! By then we had over four hundred years of the introspective conscience of the West.

While justification by faith was key for Luther, other things troubled him. The craving for reform was enhanced by the behaviour of two successive Popes. Pope Alexander (1492-1503) had passion *"for gold, women and the careers of his bastard children"*. Pope Julius II *"gratified an ornate love of war and conquest"*.[23] He rode into battle in full armour and was the Pope who set about rebuilding St Peters. But wars and an extensive rebuilding programme require a lot of money and in 1509 the Pope was planning to raise money in Germany through the sale of indulgences. Indulgences were paper certificates giving relief from punishment in Purgatory. Luther discovered this on a visit to Rome and was shocked to the core. For Luther Rome was the beast in the book of Revelation.

When a Dominican Johann Tetzel came to Germany selling these indulgences, which were oppressive to the poor, Luther went public. On 31 October 1517 he nailed his 95 theses to the Wittenberg church door. This was the normal way of giving notice of a public debate and soon Luther was caught up in a series of very public disputations. Indulgences ran counter for Luther to St Paul's view of grace and salvation. They cut across the very gospel itself as Luther had liberatingly discovered in his reading of Romans.

> *Luther's protest was quickly turned into an act of rebellion because powerful churchmen gave a heavy-handed response. He wanted to talk about grace; his opponents wanted to talk about authority. That chasm of purposes explains how an argument about a side alley of medieval soteriology (salvation) escalated into the division of Europe.*[24]

Most things do come down to a matter of authority and power. This is the issue in the contemporary dispute over same sex relations and marriage. It went to the heart of the matter in 1517 and the years following and it was why a religious protest quickly became a political revolt. German politics split between those who backed Luther and those who wanted him punished. It was the age of printing and Luther took to writing; Pamphlets abounded, up to 10,000 during the crucial Reformation years. A battle of books developed, Luther producing three in a short period of time, which were the primary texts of the Reformations. These were the *Liberty of a Christian Man, Address to the Nobility of the German Nation* and *On the Babylonian Captivity of the Church of God*. By June 1520 Luther was excommunicated from the Church. This is important to note. Luther never left the Church and the purpose of himself and others was to reform, not create schism or separate. He did publicly burn the Bill of Excommunication.

In April 1521 Luther was given a formal hearing at the Diet of Worms, the imperial parliament as it were. He was asked to recant which he refused, believing as he said neither a Pope nor councils alone. He would only be convinced from scripture or by plain reason and unless he was he would recant nothing. After Luther's death, the first editor of his collected works wrote two sentences, which he believed summed up Luther's stand at Worms. They *"have become the most famous thing Luther never said: 'Here I stand; I can do no other'"*.[25]

Luther was given safe conduct from the Diet but he was no longer safe. The Elector Friedrich arranged for Luther to go into hiding in the Wartburg Castle near Eisenach. Time was not lost here as he began his translation of the German Bible, which not only gave ordinary people the Bible in their own language, a revolutionary act, which undermined the Church authority. Luther's text shaped the German language. Political and social upheavals continued. From 1524-1525 the Peasants War or Revolt took place. If Luther could defy the Church then political authority could also be defied. Luther opposed the Peasants Revolt, surprisingly defending the social order and the rights of princes. These social disturbances were violent and the *"peasant-rebels were crushed in a sea of blood"*.[26] Luther applauded the rulers brutality in putting down the *'Farmers Revolt'* and he invoked another text from Paul, Romans 13 v 1, obedience to the superior powers whose power came from God. This has been both the most significant and abused text of the Reformation. It has had a tragic history. More violence was to follow, in fact a thirty years war. The connections between religion and violence have a long history and pose a perennial and awkward ethical question. A simplistic correlation is to be avoided, though robust analysis is required.

Luther had started a revolution, as much political as it was religious. Powers were unleashed, perhaps beyond Luther's intention and purpose. From his religious protest came the Lutheran Church, a model of Reformation which spread throughout Germany and moved north to Scandinavia.

The Reformed Reformation

Luther's protest movements didn't stop in Germany. Like a bush fire the movement spread to other parts of Europe. By 1522 there was ferment for reform in Switzerland. A key player was Ulrich Zwingli in Zurich. Zwingli challenged the Catholic Church on its organisation and doctrine. He shared Luther's abhorrence of indulgences and his liberating theology of justification by faith, but he took a different direction over the nature of Eucharist. Bread and wine were mere symbols and the Communion was a memorial. Zwingli's church polity was congregational, in that he advocated that congregations have the right to control their own life and work. Zwingli was a militarist, going into battle and in 1531 losing his life in a battle with five Catholic cantons.

Elsewhere in Switzerland another model of the Reformation was taking shape. Its roots were in the French Reformation. In 1524 William Farel published the Lord's Prayer and Creed in French, which was really a translation of Luther's Little Book of Prayers from two years earlier. Farel hoped in a 1524 letter that *"Christ will eventually visit France with his benediction"*.[27] But reforming hopes were confronted by forces of reaction. The Reformation made no great headway in France and in 1534 it hit the buffers. It was known as the *'Affair of the Placards'* and was a placard attacking the abuses of the mass, attacked papists and suggested that Christ's sacrifice in the mass was an invention and cover-up. Parisian Catholics were enraged, 200-300 people were arrested and six burned in public.

Those associated with the reform movement had to lie low and among them was Jean or John Calvin, who slipped away to Basle. There, Calvin took to writing and had ready publishers. What Calvin wrote would develop into his *Institution of the Christian Religion* in 1539. His early version was a manual of Christian orthodoxy intended for *"the French 'evangelicals' facing post-Placard repression"*.[28] The Institution became Calvin's defining work and he saw it complimenting biblical commentaries. It later became known as *The*

Institutes in 1559 and offered a summary of religion and an interpretive method for reading and study of the Bible. An important insight of Calvin's was the need to understand the author of a biblical text, so one needs to get inside the mind of Paul when reading Romans. Sacraments were instruments of nourishment and seals of our faith. Covenant featured large in Calvin's theological thought and he proclaimed a doctrine of double predestination, that God saved some and damned others. Calvin developed this theology to stop speculation about God's justice. For others it explained the division of Christendom and rationalised the divided Europe in which they lived.[29]

In 1541 Calvin was in Geneva and took control of the church there. He was a *"fugitive Frenchman, more radical than Luther, Calvin founded the most widely influential branch of Protestantism"*.[30] He worked on a constitution for the Geneva Church and the city magistrates agreed to it in 1541. It was a form of governance, collegiate governance, and Calvin believed it reflected the early Pauline church. What developed though was a theocracy in Geneva, with no aspect of civil life outside the concerns of God. The church ruled the city and Geneva gained a reputation as a godly *'New Jerusalem'*, but eventually Genevans *"felt that the Church was becoming more intrusive in their lives"*.[31] Paradoxically Calvin was creating the most democratic form of Church governance but was also setting up in Geneva a theocracy, civil society ruled by God, and not for the last time was it resisted and eventually collapsed.

Meanwhile Calvin was involved in the storm around Michael Servetus, a refugee from the Inquisition and who was considered to have unorthodox opinions, including being anti-Trinitarian. Servetus hoped that the latter would help to reunite Jews to Christianity. In 1553 Servetus was under arrest in Geneva and put on trial. Servetus made a good self-defence but Calvin brought in *"the big guns of other Reformed churches to lean on the magistrates"*.[31] On 27 October 1553, Servetus was found guilty and burned to death on the same day Calvin claimed biblical authority for the action of princes using the sword to maintain right religion.

Calvin's code for living became known in the English world as Puritanism and his covenant theology and decentralised form of church governance became known as Presbyterianism. John Knox was a friend and colleague of Calvin in Geneva and Knox brought the Reformed or Presbyterian model of the Reformation to his native Scotland, which came to the north-east in Ireland in the 1609 Plantation by James I. It was the second model of the Reformations to come to Ireland.

The English Reformation

Diarmaid MacCulloch sees in 1529-1533 the birth of Protestantism. It was really at the Diet of Speyer in 1529 that the word *'Protestant'* originated. Here a group of princes and cities united to support the movement associated with Luther and Zwingli. They issued a *'Protestatio'*, an affirmation of the reforming beliefs they shared.[32] But as the Protestant movement spread there were differences in theology and practice as well as in models of church governance. And it was impossible to separate all this from culture and politics. The Reformations, plural, had produced Protestantism, but a fractured Protestantism.

> *The years around 1530 saw a process of definition and separation, capped by three momentous fractures: unsuccessful doctrinal talks at Marburg in 1529, an abortive effort at Augsburg in 1530 to reunite the whole Church, and then in 1531 a disastrous defeat for the Swiss Reformation.*[33]

Zwingli had been butchered on the battlefield and where now was the Swiss Reformation? Fortunately Heinrich Bullinger brought back some stability. Bullinger made it a lifelong task to bridge the divide over doctrines at Marburg in 1529 and to heal a fractured Protestantism. He took to a mammoth project of European-wide letter writing, all in an effort to bring about reconciliation and better understanding. He sought to mitigate the worst divisions in belief, especially around the Eucharist. But by 1533 the Reformations were plural and Protestantism was fractured and divided, and so it has remained.

In 1529 yet another model of Reformation was introduced. That was the year when King Henry VIII of England began the process of separating the English Church from Rome. The underlying reason was hardly the most spiritual of reasons for advancing a Reformation. Henry's sexual needs were related to an heir to the English throne. It was an obsession and when his wife proved incapable of serving the succession, Henry sought a divorce. Only the Pope could grant that and he refused. Henry looked for ways of cutting ties with Rome.

Catherine of Aragon had given birth to six children, including two sons but only a girl, Mary survived. Henry believed all of this to be divine retribution and turned to the book of Leviticus, 20 v 21, as the biblical basis of a curse.

He petitioned Rome for an annulment in 1527. Being unsuccessful he sacked and imprisoned Cardinal Thomas Wolsey and replaced him with Thomas More. Meanwhile he fell in love with Anne Boleyn and he became doubly determined to get rid of Catherine and replace her, and produce heirs with Anne. He gained Parliamentary support, attacked the Catholic Church's privileges and properties. In 1531 all English clergy were asked to submit to the King and in 1532, Parliament passed the Act in Restraint of Appeals, *"which made the King of England – rather than the pope – the final legal authority in all disputes"*.[34] Now marriage annulment became a matter for English law. Anne Boleyn was already pregnant when Henry secretly married her in 1533. The Queen gave birth to a girl!

Parliament passed the Act of Supremacy in 1534 which gave the King complete control of the English Church and made any challenge to the King's ultimate authority an act of treason. Church and monarchy were one and all English Catholics had to choose between allegiance to their church and obedience to their monarch. After 1534, if Catholics rejected the Act of Supremacy their fate as traitors was death. Thomas More and Cardinal Fisher were executed.

So was born the English Reformation and the Anglican Church. Ironically Henry had earlier been declared Defender of the Faith because of his denunciation of Luther. Yet nothing much had changed for the new Anglican Church. Theology, rituals, liturgy and ethics remained. In 1536 and 1539 Articles were passed which asserted the inviolability of the Roman Mass and traditional doctrine. The real reformers were the Queen, Anne Boleyn and Archbishop of Canterbury, Thomas Cranmer. An angry Henry accused Anne of adultery, the marriage was annulled and two days later Anne was beheaded. Henry dissolved monasteries and seized properties, and in effect wiped out monasticism. Sacred buildings were pillaged and there was much destruction. *"King Henry VIII was no Protestant Reformer, however"*.[35] Others like Cranmer pushed for reform against the King's conservatism.

The English Reformation was to see itself in time as both Reformed and Catholic, and in a sense was a middle way. Like Lutheranism the Anglican Church was to become a State Church and remains so. With Henry's Tudor invasion of Ireland the Anglican Church became the first model of the Reformations to take root in Ireland. It too became the Established Church in Ireland until 1869. It was associated with Ascendancy and Penal Laws and was part of Ireland's sectarian and tragic history.

5
The Radical Left Wing
of the Reformations

The sixteenth century Reformations produced a radical minority, difficult to define and classify. They were the radicals of the Reformations and have themselves been described in the plural, the radical Reformations. *"A Revolutionary movement always produces a wing which will reform the revolution"*.[36] Those who made up this radical left wing of the Reformations were ordinary people, not with a great deal of education, in fact, saw no need for it and did not have time for academic study. Theirs was a deeply personal piety, rooted in the Bible and inspired directly by the Spirit.

> *These simple folk believed that every man (sic) had an equal right to search doctrine for himself from his Bible. They found apocalyptic visions, and the dragon cast into the bottomless pit, and they dreamed of the kingdom of heaven and of the saints, and sought to gather a little remnant of the faithful and of Babylon, and were contemptuous of the rich and the learned.*[37]

They believed that God used the common people and when Christ came, it was the poor who received the Gospel. This clearly was subversive of the church systems of power and understood the Gospel as turning the ecclesial value system on its head. But the movement was even more radical. In sixteenth century Europe, Christendom was still intact and the Protestant reformers had not gone far enough in the reform. The radical left wing of the Reformations believed that a clean break with Christendom was necessary if authentic faith and church were to be recovered. Luther and the other Protestant reformers thought they were returning to the sources of Scripture, but were stopping short of the Christian Testament model of church, which was completely separate from the State and had therefore no part in the State's power and wars.

The radicals were quickly called the Anabaptists, a pejorative term which had to do with being *'baptised twice'*. Since everyone was baptised as an infant in society, to be baptised as an adult was seen as literally a rebaptism, a being baptised twice. *"The Anabaptist label was applied to those who believed that only adults able to make a profession of faith may be baptised"*.[38] The immediate source of controversy appeared to be infant baptism but it was much deeper. And it had no resemblance to some contemporary arguments in relation to infant or adult baptism. Behind the Anabaptist position was a very different version of Christianity to the Catholic and Protestant Reformation expressions. It was for a different model of being church. It was a revolt against Christendom, which is why the Anabaptist movement was for withdrawal from the larger society.

> *This radical break from all Christian establishment has been characterised as 'a steeples Christianity' – a Christianity 'with corporate loyalties and internal disciplines transcending any earthly state and never to be subsumed under one, a people, characterised by the pursuit of holiness, separated from the world'.*[39]

The one true church consisted only of true believers, professing faith as adults and becoming part of a voluntary community. The Anabaptists were asserting a radical alternative to *'state churches'*. The baptism of infants was baptism of all into State churches, including Protestant, and that was baptism not only into the State church, but into the State itself, with all the enforced arrangements of power and obligations to fight the States wars. Baptism of adults was the radical alternative into a voluntary community of faith, which was also pacifist and against war. The Anabaptists could not find anything in the Bible to support a union of church and state. The Protestant Reformers had been encouraging the lay people to be assertive and independent in relation to the Catholic Church. Now there was a community being assertive and independent of the Protestant churches. People like Zwingli, Luther and Calvin had asserted *sola scriptura*, scripture alone and had made the Bible available to ordinary people and helped them to read the text for themselves. Now there was the surprise and shock of finding those who were reading the Bible very differently from the Reformers and challenging the heart of the Reformations. The Anabaptists were a radical movement reforming the revolution. And for most in this radical movement non-violence was an essential part of faith in practice and their baptism as adult believers was a sign of their practice of non-violence and withdrawal from the church-state society, i.e. Christendom.

Not surprisingly both Catholic and Protestant traditions responded with violence to the Anabaptists. Drownings were thought a fitting end for those who subverted Christendom and its political power through their baptism of adult believers. In the case of Protestants, it was Protestants killing Protestants.

The Protestant killing began in Zurich. Ulrich Zwingli, the Zurich reformer was confronted with radical dissent and, true to form, dealt with it violently. On the 5 January 1527, Felix Mantz, an Anabaptist reformer, was taken out to the town fish market, forced into a boat and taken out into the river where he was strapped to a pole and then thrown into the freezing waters and drowned. He *"earned himself the sad distinction of being the first Protestant to be martyred by other Protestants. His crime was that of rebaptising".*[40] Even though his last words as he disappeared into the depths of the river were those of Jesus at the moment of his death, *"Into your hands, O Lord, I command my spirit"*, this was described by Heinrich Bullinger, Zwingli's successor in Zurich, as foolishness! Mantz's real crime of heresy was for insisting that the church conform to the church in the Acts of the Apostles and Paul's Letters, that it's members were believing, baptising adults, and that church and state should therefore be separate. That was too much for the Protestant Reformers in Zurich. If the Protestant Reformations were insisting on *sola scriptura*, scripture alone, then the Anabaptists were challenging the consistency of Luther, Zwingli and Calvin's claim. The violent response of the Protestant Reformers to the Anabaptists meant that the Reformers were not willing to accept their own logic. *Sola scriptura* couldn't deliver after all!

What Was Radical?

Before looking at some of the high profile Anabaptists, it would be helpful to examine the content of their *'radical'* stance. There were five features described by Eire:

• *Belief in the church as having fallen and disappeared at some point in early Christian history.*
• *Belief in an essential, unbridgeable chasm between Christians and 'the world'.*
• *Belief in strictly voluntary Christianity, and in a church composed only of believers.*
• *Rejection of infant baptism as an earmark of the compulsory, fallen, territorial churches.*
• *Belief in the freedom of the human will, and in the role of human effort toward salvation.*[41]

What this really meant was the rejection of the Protestant Reformers and what they were protesting or affirming as insufficient and incomplete. The nearest this Anabaptist movement came to a formal confession of faith was in 1527, the same year that Mantz was drowned. A month later Michael Sattler, a former Benedictine monk wrote a confession that was agreed at Schleitheim, a town north of Zurich. Known as the Schleitheim Articles or Confession, they proclaimed adult baptism, separation from the world, condemned the use of force, going to the law, becoming a magistrate or taking of oaths. This was the rejection of Christendom, the rejection of the marriage of church and state. Some of the seven major principles agreed affirmed that:

• *Baptism and church membership are strictly for believing adults only.*
• *The Eucharist is the ultimate sign of exclusion, reserved for those who do not sin, for Christians 'cannot at the same time partake and drink of*

the cup of the Lord and the cup of devils'.

- *There is to be no mingling with 'the evil that the devil planted in the world', and this applies not only to all sinful behaviour, but also all 'diabolical weapons of violence-such as sword, armour and the like'.*
- *Christians are never to hold any civil offices, for all earthly governments rely on violence for discipline, and 'the sword is ordained of God outside the perfection of Christ'.*[42]

Some of this may seem very exclusive and separatist, but the Anabaptists were working out a faith that they believed, recovered the earliest church and radically broke the diabolical connection between church and state. Violence was at the heart of this relationship and within Christendom, the church had legitimised and blessed the state's wars, armies and weapons. To be part of this violence and come to the Eucharist was to partake and drink *'the cup of devils'.* Separation from the church-state apparatus was the rejection of violence and the *"diabolical weapons of violence".* With a theology like this, the Anabaptists were always going to be seen as a threat to social and political stability.

Not all Anabaptists were so radical about violence and war. In Zwickau in Germany there were prophets, among them Thomas Müntzer, who were apocalyptic activists. They had come to believe in the apocalyptic visions in the Bible, dragons being cast into the lake, literalised them and believed that they were God's prophets to cast down the powers of the world and build the New Jerusalem on earth. Müntzer died in the Peasants Revolt of 1525 and his legacy lived on in the radicalised activities of his followers. Their commitment, as was his, was to prophecy, apocalypticalism and revolution. This led to the Münster debacle. Münster, a city near the Dutch border, was already a centre of radical religious dissidents. The city had been declared the New Jerusalem in 1534 and a leader declared that the *'godless'* would be put to death if they refused to join the new baptismal covenant. Many left the city but those who remained were forcibly re-baptised. Violence reigned, a direct consequence of the apocalyptic visions of

Thomas Müntzer. The Anabaptist New Jerusalem was destroyed after a fierce battle in 1535. Münster was destroyed. *"The tragedy of Münster was a consequence not only of the leaders' megalomania but also of the followers conviction that the Bible as interpreted by their leaders was to be literally followed".*[43] *Sola scriptura* could also be violently dangerous!

There was never another attempt to establish a New Jerusalem, but the Münster debacle led to developments that strengthened the anti-violence and peace emphasis of the radical left wing of the Reformations. Two leaders stand out.

Jacob Hutter died in 1536, did much to stabilise the struggling Anabaptist communities of Moravia. Taking a characteristic of the Acts of the Apostles church seriously, he sold his house and goods and established communistic communities. Goods and production were shared and there was an egalitarianism, which had something of the earlier monastic movement behind it. A common life and a common goal were shared. Hutter was not for individualism, but a *"covenanted community of families that claimed to be the church itself, outside of which there was no salvation".*[44] This was church as a model of the household of faith characterised by non-violence and a communism of love. Hutter was put to death in 1536. Hutterite Anabaptists later found life and freedom in North America.

Better known was Menno Simons, a former priest who died in 1561. His brother died in the Münster violence. Menno emerged as a leader of the Dutch and north German Anabaptists, who *"were gathered into voluntary communities separate from the established civic and religious world".*[45] This was difficult because it meant refusing military service and the paying of certain taxes. Being an Anabaptist was not easy. The Münster debacle had a huge impact throughout Europe, increasing persecution and suffering. Menno Simons strongly emphasised pacifism and articulated an Anabaptist position close to the Schleitheim Articles. Menno held a middle ground, marginalising the extremes in the Anabaptist movement. In the situation of Anabaptist disarray, Menno brought greater theological rigour and a stronger ethical code to shared life. He strengthened community, provided greater cohesion and a more distinctive identity. All of this was important for a persecuted minority of people. *"His pacifist stance also worked wonders in terms of public relations, especially for a separatist minority, helping Anabaptists regain the trust of their neighbours after the spectacle of Münster. And it was their behaviour, not just their thinking, that made Mennonites seem acceptable".*[46]

The Anabaptists following Menno Simons were a distinctive group, very different from the classical Protestants and the Catholic Church. More than any other they embodied the radical left wing of the Reformations. At the heart of the Mennonites was not only the practice of radical non-violence but the power of transformation and moral empowerment in the lives of followers of Christ. They too found it difficult in a Europe divided between Protestant and Catholic. Persecution led to a Mennonite exodus to North America. They were never to be anything other than a minority but as such they have become the main historic peace church. In the late twentieth century their witness to peace as truly apostolic has at last been recognised by the Protestant and Catholic churches that made life extremely difficult for them during the sixteenth century Reformations and beyond. With Christendom now dead (not altogether recognised by all in the West) the radical Reformation with its radical non-violence and radical peace is a voice for the twenty-first century. They were ahead of their time. Perhaps their day has come.

6
The Catholic Reformation

So much attention has been given to the Protestant Reformations that it is possible to overlook the fact that reform also took place in the Catholic Church. Protestant reformers were not the only people attempting to reform the Church, nor were they the only people taking risks and suffering for their reform efforts. The power of Christendom was such that any person pushing for reform was in trouble and often experienced violent opposition. Attempts at reform are always perceived by those in power as a threat and an undermining of the status quo. Notable reformers within the Catholic Church stand out.

Carlo Borromeo was the archbishop of Milan whose reforming efforts were totally opposed by his clergy. On 26 October 1569 as he knelt in the cathedral during evening prayer, he was shot in the back by one of his priests. The bishop survived and despite his plea for mercy and expression of forgiveness, the priest was executed. He had already survived an earlier attempt on his life by the canons of a church and their mob of supporters.

In Spain bishop Francisco Robuster y Sala fled his diocese after three shots were fired at him. He had the support of his clergy but the canons of his cathedral were from wealthy families and there was an intense power struggle with potential for violence that led to armed guards on the bishop's house. Priests and canons were armed, such was the threat of religious reform.

St John of the Cross was a Carmelite monk who wrote love poems to God. He too was a reformer though not a bishop. He was imprisoned in 1577, held in appalling conditions, flogged and beaten regularly and only survived by escaping in 1578. The rest of his life was spent on the run from those who did not want reform, even though his reform plan was backed by the Pope and had originated with St. Teresa of Avila. *"And these are only three of hundreds of similar stories that could be told of reformers who met violent resistance. 'Some Reformation' one might be tempted to say".[47]*

The ferment of reform was also within the Catholic Church and in trying to understand and evaluate it, it needs to be noted that it was a very long and complex process. It runs parallel to the Protestant Reformations but in one sense, goes beyond them. The lengthy process of reform can be dated to the end of the fourteenth century. From 1517 when Luther nailed his theses to the Wittenberg Church door to the opening of the reforming Council of Trent, Catholic reform was uncoordinated. The Council of Trent met between 1545-1563 and reformers pushed the Church leadership to come up with real reform. From 1563-1618 the reforms of Trent were implemented and Catholics took back territories that had been in the hands of Protestants.[48] The issue of territoriality is a reminder that in the Christendom context there was no dividing line between religion and political power. Faith and territory were inseparable.

The pressure for Catholic reform pre-dates Luther, but when he did burst on the scene, one of the first to oppose him was Cardinal Cajetan at the Diet of Augsburg in 1518. Cajetan could do nothing to stop Luther and the blaze that was spreading rapidly in Germany. Cajetan set about repudiating Luther's theology through very learned Latin treatises, but Luther's appeal was to the common people and Cajetan was writing theology way beyond street level. There were those who, like Luther, could take theology to the street level. One such person was bishop Jacopo Sadoleto who in 1539 wrote a letter to Geneva. John Calvin refuted the letter publicly and in print. Some fifty years later St Francis de Sales wrote leaflets against Protestant teachings in Geneva and along with sermons and unceasing pastoral care, de Sales is reputed to have converted some 72,000 Protestants from the Geneva region back to the Catholic faith. Three other high profile reformers are worth noting.

Giovanni Pietro Carafa was from Naples and became disillusioned with his Church career and corrupt papal finances. Between 1514-1617 he founded an Oratory of Divine Love in Rome. This was a

trend of the time enhancing pious activism and renewing religious
orders. The Oratories became important foundations. Carafa by 1524
had founded a congregation of clergy under special vows. This was a
serious minded articulate clergy, not unlike the new forms of
Protestant clergy, though with total loyalty to Rome.

From another Roman Oratory came Gasparo Contarini, regionally
Venetian. Contarini had founded an Oratory in Venice but in 1511
he had a spiritual crisis similar to Luther's some few years earlier.
When Luther emerged proclaiming his justification by faith,
Contarini understood what he was saying. Recognising the liberating
truth of Luther's experience and teaching, Contarini devoted the rest
of his life in the Church to bringing about reconciliation between the
opposing sides. In 1541 Contarini was a papal delegate to the
Colloquy at Regensburg, where he was involved in direct negotiations
with German Protestant theologians. He actually succeeded in getting
an agreed statement on justification by faith. The talks though, broke
down, which left Contarini being portrayed as a dangerous
compromiser.[49] Contarini died in 1542 in suspicious circumstances,
some claimed he was poisoned by enemies.

In the 1530s Contarini had been introduced to Reginald Pole, an
exiled Englishman with a better hereditary claim to the English
throne than Henry VIII. Unfortunately for Pole he took sides with
Catherine of Aragon, which forced him to flee from Henry who had
sponsored his Italian education. Pole was cultured and had sufficient
income to live comfortably in Italian exile. His strong sense of duty
and a thoughtful, introspective piety made him a major player in
Italian theological ferment.[50] Both Pole and Contarini held to the
centrality of the role of grace by faith in the Christian life, and
recognised that Luther was on the same theological wavelength.

Diarmaid MacCulloch draws attention to a significant woman in
the Catholic Reformation, which shows that the ferment was not just
about elite, clerical, male spirituality. She was Angela Merici from
Brescia. She made it her life's purpose to encourage single women to

practice the religious life within their own homes. These women were to be unmarried, not even widows could participate. Influential was a fourth century martyr, St Ursula. So began the Ursulines *"thirsting to help a rather startled and intimidated male-run Church"*.[51] This work was among the poor and the education of children where men refused to go. The Pope gave them a Rule, not unlike that of the Augustinians. Despite the centralised control efforts of Borromeo, the otherwise reform-minded archbishop of Milan, the Merici vision of individuality was too strong and had produced strong-minded women, enough to ignore the Church hierarchy's alternative plans.

The Popes of the Catholic Reformation were a rather mixed group. Florentine Girolamo Savonarola was a revivalist preacher who identified Pope Alexander VI as the antichrist and the Church as a prostitute Church. In 1497 Alexander excommunicated Savonarola and a year later the city turned on him and hanged him. But there was growing belief that something had to be done about these corrupt Popes. Reform minded Catholics were on the increase and a key figure was Erasmus of Rotterdam, who from his humanist perspective savagely attacked Church corruption. Alexander had been succeeded by Julius II, a belligerent, worldly and warring Pope. The growing clamour for reform was failing but Julius was forced to call the Fifth Lateran Council in 1512. The Pope controlled everything, including the agenda. He died before the Council completed its work and was succeeded by Leo X, who was only thirty-seven years of age. Leo was more peaceful and expectations for reform rose. In 1512 Leo created thirty-one new cardinals and in the same year Luther produced his theses against indulgences. Pope Julius and Pope Leo had issued the indulgences to help fund the rebuilding of St Peters. The indulgences were corrupt and Luther's was not the only voice raised against them. Luther's protest roused the poor, who were the primary victims of the system, promising liberation from a system that oppressed and impoverished them. In 1525 the German peasants revolted, quoting Luther, who disowned the revolutionary readings of his message. Pope Leo failed to see how serious things were and then tried to silence

Luther. Leo issued a Papal Bull in 1520 condemning Luther and excommunicating him.

Pope Leo was succeeded in 1522 by Hadrian VI, a reformer. He had already been involved in reform movements for biblical studies, clerical education and improved preaching.[52] Hadrian intended to reform the Curia but he died a year later, a disappointed Pope. Clement VII became Pope and his papal office was characterised by intense political power struggles, which came to a head in 1527 when a German army sacked Rome, killing 4000 people and claiming Luther's authority. It took a decade for the city to recover. Western Christendom was becoming deeply divided and religious civil war was the order of the day.

Into this religious crisis came Pope Paul III, a sixty seven year old experienced cardinal. But he belonged to the school of corruption. Known in Roman circles as *'Cardinal Petticoat'*, because of his mistress and four children, he built himself a magnificent palace. His first two appointments as cardinals were his two teenage grandsons. And yet it was Pope Paul who gave the Catholic Church the impetus and direction for internal reform, missing until then. In 1513 his relationship with his mistress had ended and unusually he was ordained priest.

Associated with reform, therefore, Pope Paul was now pushing for a Council. Against opposition from cardinals who feared change beginning with them, Paul pushed ahead. The Lutherans, though, refused to attend a Council on Italian soil and one presided over by the Pope. Emperor Charles wanted practical reforms. The Pope wanted both doctrinal and practical reforms and he would preside. In December 1545 the Council of Trent was launched, Trent being in the Italian Alps, and acceptable to the Lutherans because it was nominally in imperial territory.

Pope Paul appointed new cardinals, the first being Gasparo Contarini. Contarini became a guiding hand, which enabled the Pope to bring to Rome *"a remarkable circle of reformers, all of whom he made cardinals*".[53] These included Reginald Pole, the reforming bishop of Verona, Giberti and Carafa from Naples. These reformers, highlighted earlier, were now part of a Reform Commission, tasked with producing a report on the ills of the Church and ways forward. Significantly, none of the Curia were members of the Commission. In 1537 they produced their explosive report. The Curia tried to block it, it was leaked to the outside world and in 1538 Luther published it in German.

Contarini and Pole believed Luther to be sinfully wrong on ecclesiastical authority and sacraments, but were certain he was right in relation to justification and salvation by faith in Christ, rather than by good works. Contarini and Pole *"helped and worked for reconciliation with the Lutherans"*.[54] Division came through Carafa who believed in the urgent need for reform as moral, institutional and spiritual, but rejected Luther's teaching as heretical. Contarini and Pole were eventually seen as *"a crypto-Protestant fifth column within the Church"*.[55] Carafa called for a Roman Inquisition and in 1542 six inquisitors were appointed with powers of arrest and scrutiny across Europe. Paul had already passed a Papal Bull approving the Society of Jesus with Ignatius Loyola as its first general. The Jesuits became the most powerful element of the Catholic Reformation.

In December 1545 the Council met at Trent and lasted for another five pontificates, including Carafa as Pope Paul IV (1555-59) at seventy-nine years of age. Trent began by discussing the theology of justification. Duffy's point is well made that *"In a sense Trent came a generation too late, a generation during which the split in the Church had widened and hardened"*.[56] If only movement for reform had begun earlier or a Council had been called earlier, some reconciliation may have been realised, but when positions harden, reconciliation becomes difficult, if not impossible. Trent did produce clarity on a number of issues for the Catholic Church. The issues were all contested; justification, seven sacraments, transubstantiation, and purgatory. Late-medieval Catholic interpretation was eliminated and practical reform emerged. There was a new system of training for clergy. Clergy were to be better educated, more moral and professional. Preaching and teaching were given new emphasis. *"The Church after Trent would be better organised, better staffed, more clerical, more vigilant, more repressive, altogether a more formidable institution".*[57] The reform movement did concentrate authority in the hands of the papacy and in the final sessions of Trent in 1562-1563, many bishops wanted the Council to issue strong decrees on the *'divine right'* of bishops. What that meant, though, was that a bishop's authority was directly from God and not from the Pope. The Jesuit theologians were behind that position. The Council ended in 1563 with its reforms still needing implementation. The next seven years saw a confirmation of decrees on a revised Index of Prohibited Books, a reformed missal, breviary and a catechism along with other service books. The new seminaries to produce better educated and trained clergy were crucial to reform implementation. The clergy who emerged from them were *"fundamental to the recovery of Catholicism in Europe and beyond".*[58]

The Council of Trent was one of the most highly significant moments in all Catholic history. The Council *"reformed the Church from top to bottom, setting the course Catholicism would follow for the following four centuries".*[59] The success of Trent was due to individuals, committed to the implementation of reforms, *"popes, cardinals, bishops, abbots, monks, priests, nuns, and lay people who struggled to bring about change against entrenched interests, financial obstacles, suspicion of their motives and hostility toward innovation".*[60] This is the challenge for every movement for reform.

7
Women and the Reformations

It is only in relatively recent decades that attention has been given to the role or status of women during the Reformations. This is no doubt because women in church and society have become more significant in a time when feminism has entered a third phase, equality laws have been enhanced and there is a greater awareness of the pervasive nature of patriarchy in the late twentieth and early twenty-first centuries. Yet there are still serious gaps in salaries for women and men, often for the same jobs, there are glass ceilings that stubbornly remain and most of the widespread domestic abuse and violence is against women. The church remains a powerhouse for men, even though women outnumber men in relation to religious practice. The Pope has recently ruled out ordination of women as a final verdict. In the Protestant churches in Ireland where women are ordained they remain a minority and are likely to be so for the foreseeable future. There are still those who find it unacceptable, making their case on biblical grounds as strongly as the Catholic Church makes its case on the grounds of tradition. Perhaps all are making the case on the grounds of tradition which has very little if anything to do with the practice of Jesus and the Paul of his seven authentic letters. A biblical case against women's ordination can be made from the probably-not Pauline writings, Colossians and Ephesians, and the definitely-not Pauline writings, I and II Timothy and Titus. The real problem is that the biblical evidence is in dispute with itself, which raises questions about the Protestant Reformations mantra, *sola scriptura*. With the growing awareness of the pervasive history of patriarchy, the rule of the male or father, and the demand for gender justice, as well as the recognition that sexual identity takes multiple forms, the Reformations became a focus on how well women fared in the sixteenth century. After all it has, with justice, been described as a revolutionary century and the Reformations as a revolution. But was it a revolution for women?

The Protestant Reformations claimed to be recovering the authenticity of the early church. This was radical in that it was going back to the roots of the gospel and was therefore liberating. But did it recover good news for women and was there a liberation for women into the kind of equality and freedom of Jesus in relation to women and in Paul's community where there was no longer male or female, slave or free, Jew or Greek? The radical left wing of the Protestant Reformations had already made it clear that the classical reformers were not radical enough. There was not a clean break between church and state and the faith and violence that was an inseparable part of Christendom. Was there also a failure to break with patriarchy?

Up to the sixteenth century, women had two important forms of representation in the Christian Church. They could enter religious or monastic life and play a significant role as Angela Merici, founder of the Ursulines did, or St Teresa of Avila who was free enough to formulate a reform plan, which was backed by the Pope. The other form was a significant identification with Mary, the mother of Jesus. In the Catholic Church marriage was a sacrament, a means of grace and holiness and a high estate, but the alternative was there for those who did not have a vocation to marriage and motherhood. Theology got around the motherhood of Mary by creating a tradition of perpetual virginity. Contradictory or illogical or not, women had Mary as model and a vocation in religious orders with chastity included as a higher form of holiness. The Protestant Reformations closed off these two forms to women. For the Reformers women could reach salvation through childbirth, which was after all what the I Timothy text said. Mary was demoted as an icon or model of faith, despite Luke's Gospel! Where did this leave Protestant women?

It de-institutionalized the church and the household of faith became the family, and not just the family, but the patriarchal family where the father ruled and had responsibility for the spiritual development of wife, children and servants. With the centrality of the *Word* and the preaching of the Word to worship, there was no place for women preachers, but within the home, subordinate to husband and father, the wife was the educator of boys and girls, teaching them to read the Bible. Women were passive readers of the *Word*, but not proclaimers in public.

With no way into a religious order, an unmarried woman was regarded with suspicion. The only vocation to ministry, with all monasteries dissolved in Protestantism was within the patriarchal family. The Protestant Reformations made family central, the high-water mark of spiritual possibility, but reinforced the patriarchal family. It was not a return to pure biblical practice, but as with Colossians, Ephesians and the Pastoral Letters, an accommodation to Greco-Roman cultural patterns, the earliest Greek practice reaching back to the origins of patriarchy in the ancient Babylonian culture which predated even the Hebrew Bible.

Perhaps the most high profile Reformation woman was Katherine von Bora, who had been a nun from childhood, but had left the convent to marry the former monk, Martin Luther. They were happily married, Luther referring to her as his *hausfrau* in the many letters he wrote to a circle of friends. They in turn loved Kathe. Both had made a stark departure from the Catholic ideal of priesthood on the one hand and chastity in a religious order on the other. They had a deep affection for each other and their children. They each missed the other deeply when he travelled. Kathe was an expert brewer of beer and sex was mutually enjoyed.

As part of Luther's famous table talk he once complained to Kathe; *"You persuade me of anything you will, you have the domain. In the household I concede to you the governance, saving only my right"*.[61] It sounds laudable but Luther goes on immediately to say that the rule of women never accomplished anything good and when *"Eve persuaded him that he was a Lord above God, he thereby spoiled it all. We have that to thank you women for…"*.[62] Luther did believe that Eve was vulnerable as a woman to temptation, was a lesser being to Adam, less rational and more emotional, and after the *Fall*, all her fault really, she was, like all women, subordinate to husbands.

It is not altogether insignificant that Kathe always addressed Luther as *'Sir Doctor'*, while he always used the first name. While he did sometimes consult Kathe on church matters, her life was entirely focused on him and their children. She was bereft when he died in 1546. She died in 1552 after a fall from a wagon at fifty-nine years of age. Though she was something of a helper in the Reformation cause, Kathe's real recognition was *"confined to the household and the giving of hospitality and shelter as well as childbirth"*.[63]

John Calvin had two significant approaches to women. Steeped as the Protestant Reformers were in Renaissance humanism, Calvin came to believe that women were educable. He encouraged the education of women, which was more ideal than practice. Yet the ideal was not original to Calvin as a reformer. Erasmus and others had advocated the education of women earlier and Calvin was no doubt aware of them. Calvin insisted on catechesis for children which would have included girls, though Catholic convents provided education for girls in Geneva long before the Genevan reformers got around to it. Even though Calvin was for the education of girls, there was in practice no equality of opportunity with the need to educate boys a length ahead. Also the education of women had no public role. Its purpose was to *"incubate the private virtues 'appropriate to the weaker sex'. A vernacular but not a Latin education meant that reformers were not innovators of women's education but populizers"*.[64]

In relation to marriage the Reformers, like Calvin, revaluated marriage by putting marriage above celibacy. It became a vocation, a calling, religiously significant. The family became *"the primary context in which faith and obedience is to be exercised"*. Furthermore women had a priestly responsibility for intercession, marriage was a means of procreation and remedy against fornication, and is for mutual love and companionship.[65] Where Calvin was innovative was in relation to the laws of divorce and adultery where women were less free than men. Calvin set about reforming Genevan laws and in 1545 *"the woman's right to divorce an unfaithful spouse was affirmed as a conscious departure from long standing legal tradition"*, according to a draft. Attempts were made to block this change but Calvin was persistent and it became law in 1561. Calvin was also intolerant of wife abuse.[66] On Calvin's part it was a relative egalitarianism but within a generation Geneva dropped the more egalitarian divorce legislation. Hierarchialism in marriage was returned. For the reformers patriarchal marriage was a God-given blessing that needs only to be humanized by greater love and respect. Nevertheless, women must remain subject to their husbands as head of the household.[67]

The Reformations took place in a century when attitudes to sex and sexuality were oppressively negative. A late fifteenth century confessional manual listed seven ways a husband and wife could sin. Those included engaging in unnatural acts and positions, contraception, coitus interruptus, sodomy and onanism, and having sex for sheer pleasure.[68] The Reformers rejected the negative attitude. There was no theological claim that to abstain from sex was meritorious, because that was works-righteousness. There was no superior status for celibacy and nothing in the Scripture to advocate it. Celibacy was unnatural and warped personalities and led to all kinds of sexual perversions.[69]

It was on issues of sexuality and marriage that the Protestant Reformations brought major changes. Married life in all its challenges was accepted and celibacy was rejected and the Catholic teaching on sex and marriage seen as a total inversion of values.

Protestant clergy stressed familial love, mutual respect and a very patriarchal authority structure in which the father, or paterfamilias, ruled his household with firm and unquestionable authority. Ideally, every father was to be both lord and pastor of his household… As far as wives were concerned, all Protestants agreed with the Apostle Paul, insisting that they should be submissive and obedient to their husbands. (Colossians 3:18-21) They also called on wives to dedicate themselves to their husbands and households.[70]

Pauline authorship was unquestioned in the sixteenth century and the lack of critical awareness gave Paul a bad name in relation to women. It is now recognized that Colossians is later than Paul, is the work perhaps of a Pauline school, living at a time when Paul's egalitarian ethic was giving way to the cultural norms of Greco-Roman society where patriarchy and hierarchy ruled. The Reformers revaluation of marriage is only one of many revaluations and modifications in history, often for financial reasons rather than spiritual ones, indeed the real financial reason often under a veneer of spirituality. Today revaluation is again under way and the shape and role of family is also changing. The Reformers interpretation of the early Genesis texts, which they read through an Augustinian prism, has also been questioned.

In the sixteenth century the Council of Trent reaffirmed the superiority of celibacy and virginity for Catholics. The celibate priesthood was still in place as were monasteries and convents. The attitude to sex did not change, with sex and sin closely connected and marriage was for procreation primarily, in fact, first and last, and it was indissoluble, no matter how dysfunctional the union.[71]

Where all this takes us in the twenty-first century is a contentious issue. Attitudes to sex, marriage and family are again in ferment and churches are generally fearful and deeply divided. Sexism, misogyny and homophobia are unacceptable ethically and in relation to being human.

The impact of the Reformations on women then was not as contentious as it is now. Did Protestant or Catholic women come out best? Protestants now, or some at least will point to liberation in contrast to the continued oppression of Catholic women. But it was not and is not so simple. Sister Jerónima de la Asunción, an early seventeenth century Catholic had the possibility of leading missions to Asia, of founding and running schools, hospitals and orphanages. Such a woman needed a great deal of self-confidence to take on such a mission in a very alien culture and she was able to do it. She was a woman in charge and by all accounts a Catholic nun to be reckoned with![72] Liberation of women took different forms. It still does in the new challenges found in gender justice in the twenty-first century.

8
The Sectarianisation of the Reformations in Ireland

There was too much in Irish political life to ensure that the Protestant Reformations would not be a success in Ireland. In October 2017 the 500th anniversary of the Protestant Reformations will be commemorated. But in 500 years Protestantism remains a minority expression of Christian faith on the island of Ireland, with most of the adherents located in what is now Northern Ireland, and even then largely in the counties of Down and Antrim. Even a century after Luther had nailed his 95 theses to the Wittenberg church door, it was clear that Protestantism was not going to take hold in Ireland. *Ireland became the only country in Reformation Europe where, over a century, a monarchy with a consistent religious agenda failed to impose it on its subjects: an extraordinary failure on the part of the Tudors and Stuarts*.[73] Politics and strong, ancient traditions and culture stood in the way. Ireland was a troubled land since the Normans arrived in the twelfth century. Strictly speaking, this was colonisation by the Plantagenets, making Ireland part of an Anglo-French empire. History read backwards, as it often is in Ireland, meant that Irish nationalists saw this as the beginning of English involvement in Ireland. That is something of an over-simplification and tends to ignore the complexity of the time, which included a deposed Irish King bringing the Normans to Ireland in an attempt to regain his lost power. It also ignores the role of Pope Adrian and his Papal Bull granting Ireland to the Plantagenet King and the process of Romanisation that brought to an end the Celtic Church and replaced it with a centralised, Roman diocesan system, which early in the next century did not even have an Irish bishop.

It was in the sixteenth century, the century of the Reformations, that Ireland became England's first colony. The Tudors invaded Ireland and Henry VIII became initially *'Lord of Ireland'*. In 1541 he took the title *'King of Ireland'*, which also meant being *'head of the Church'* in Ireland.

This meant not only English political rule but also an Established Church. Marital politics had brought the Reformation to England when Henry broke off the connection to Rome and the Pope. Now the English model of the Reformation had arrived in Ireland. Administratively Ireland was closely tied to England and Henry set about the seizure of monastic land, the dissolution of the monasteries, at least half of Ireland's monasteries, and the property of Irish noble, Thomas Fitzgerald, Lord Offaly. When the Irish Parliament in 1536-1537 had accepted the Act of Supremacy, imposing on penalty Henry's Kingship and control and his headship of the Established Church and that Church's control in Ireland, Fitzgerald had led a rebellion in protest. The rebellion was put down which led to increased English control. Like all colonisers, the English thought poorly of the Irish, portraying Ireland as a *'dark corner'*. Yet Henry adopted a strategy of granting titles to Irish nobles and land grants if they accepted the Act of Supremacy. The English Reformation had come to Ireland on the back of the Tudor invasion and colonisation of Ireland. Resentful and disempowered or dominated Irish were never likely to accept the Protestant faith. If anything it would and did increase their loyalty to Catholicism.

Ironically, it might have been different. Ireland just might have become Protestant if Catholic Queen Mary had survived and the English monarchy had remained Catholic. It was Mary who implemented a plantation of English settlers in Counties Leix and Offaly. The two counties were known as Kings and Queens Counties until Ireland was partitioned in 1921. Mary's husband, was Philip of Spain and they were successful colonisers in Central and South America.[74] The chances were that the Irish would have resented and rebelled against Catholic Mary and become Protestant in the process. But it was Elizabeth I who succeeded Mary, restoring Protestantism and her own Act of Supremacy and Act of Uniformity. For the majority of Irish, Gaelic and English-speaking, Catholicism was a strong identity marker over against the English and also the Established Protestantism.

The Established Protestant Church was not only part of governance in Ireland, it developed and created Penal Laws, designed to control Catholicism. There was nothing unusual about Established Churches and Penal Laws in the Europe of this time. The difference was that on the European mainland, Established Churches were the Churches of the majority with Penal Laws imposed against minorities. In Ireland it was the other way round. The Established Church was the Church of the minority 10%, imposing Penal Laws on the majority.

The Elizabethan Acts of Supremacy and Uniformity were an imposition of state and church control. There was also the strategy of religious conversion. Elizabeth founded Trinity College Dublin to train clergy to be an army of evangelists converting the Catholic Irish to the true faith. Whatever Trinity was to later become, its founding purpose was a spectacular failure. The Protestant-Catholic tension in Trinity continued until the early 1970s.

The failure of Protestantism to take root in Ireland, except as a publicly established Church, was reflected in the first distinctively Protestant document, the 1615 Articles of the Church of Ireland. The Anglicans on the other side of the Irish Sea had Thirty-Nine Articles, the Irish came up with 104 Articles and with two very distinctive differences. The Irish Articles were more Calvinistic than the English Articles. Catholicism was tyrannical and the Pope was the Antichrist. The Irish Articles were more anti-Catholic in tone. The biggest difference was in the doctrine of double predestination. God had elected some to salvation and other to damnation. The Irish Protestants knew who the damned were and God had predestined the Catholics to hell. It was a neat rationalisation of failure to convert the Catholic Irish and a dogmatic assertion of theology as a cover for the insecurity of a minority, who deep down knew they would never be anything else.

These Articles were part of the ethos and spirit of the Established Church's new seminary to train its clergy as an evangelistic army. In 1634 the Irish Articles gave way to the Thirty-Nine Articles. *"The Irish Articles were not actually repealed, but left to wither…"* [75]

Catholic Ireland was aware of the Catholic Reformation and that one of the reforms from Trent was the establishment of seminaries to train a more educated, theologically and spiritually aware and more moral clergy. Unlike the Established Church of Ireland, Penal Laws did not allow for a Catholic equivalent of Trinity College Dublin. The Catholic Reformation Irish took to building Irish colleges in Europe. John Lee from Waterford founded the first college in Paris. Waterford was a key centre of the Catholic Reformation in Ireland and it was a significant port connecting Irish trade to France and Spain. Lee was one of the Old English and was part of a network of mercantile families who were fervent supporters and astute agents of the Catholic Reformation in Ireland. Lee founded his Irish college in 1578 and was followed by Thomas White of Clonmel in Spain (1592), John Howling in Lisbon (1593) and Christopher Cusack who founded four Irish colleges in France.[76]

In order to implement Trent, the Irishmen had borrowed money from European courts and in the sixteenth and seventeenth centuries, Irish colleges were founded in many European centres, including one in Rome and three in Belgium. Meanwhile, the Established Church belatedly published a Gaelic New Testament in 1603 and Gaelic prayer book in 1608, but the failure of Protestantism in Ireland to become the religion of the people was already evident. In 1608 the Irish Privy Council was complaining that the influx of newly trained Catholic clergy from the European seminaries was becoming a torrent. They were landing secretly in Irish ports and dispersing quietly throughout the country.

Penal Laws were strengthened in 1704 by Queen Anne to *"prevent the further growth of Popery".* These not only imposed further restrictions on Catholics, the Penal Laws were also imposed on Presbyterians. This crowning piece of legislation *"…represented the final dismantling of the terms agreed between the forces of King James and those of King William at Limerick in 1691".*[77] King William found Penal Laws rather distasteful but his daughter Queen Anne thought otherwise and her Penal Code was enacted for thirty-nine years.

The Catholic Reformation provided a focus for opposition in Ireland, which continued to develop. The Catholic Church in Ireland developed into a very powerful institution in the mid-nineteenth century through the leadership of Cardinal Paul Cullen. Cullen was a product of Rome and an ultramontane, committed to theological orthodoxy and the absolute power of the Pope in all matters. He created a reforming synod in Thurles in 1851 and restructured the Irish Catholic Church. It became a powerful institution, authoritarian, produced a strong clericalism and a Church involved in every aspect of Irish life. Cullen was against fraternisation with Protestants. He was influential as the drafter of the final decree on papal infallibility promulgated at Vatican Council I in 1870.

The powerful Irish Catholic institution was that with which Sinn Fein became closely aligned after the landslide election victory in 1918. The Catholic Church continued its political domination of Irish politics until the 1960s when the *Cullenised* Church began to lose its political and public power. It was Cullen's Church that Ulster Protestants feared during the Home Rule crisis, though their main objection to Home Rule in the Presbyterian inspired Ulster Covenant was the fear of economic loss that a Home Rule parliament would bring about in the north east.

After 1609 a second Reformation model arrived in Ireland. James I drew up the Articles of Plantation for Ulster in order to control the troublesome province and replace the false religion of Catholicism with the true faith of Protestantism. Ulster was the last bastion of Gaelic independence in Ireland and Elizabeth's forces had just ended a nine years war with the latest rebellious army of Hugh O'Neill of Tyrone. O'Neill had finally been defeated at the battle of Kinsale in 1601 and with the Earl of Tyrconnell had left Ulster in the Flight of the Earls in 1607. James produced his Plantation Articles to deal with Catholic rebellion once and for all.

Welsh and English settlers arrived in Ulster but the majority of those planted were Scottish and Presbyterian. The Plantation of Ulster, the earlier entrepreneurial plantation and the legislated plantation brought the Reformed or Calvinist model of Reformation to the north-east of Ireland. The Plantation was not as complete as James had hoped for. Presbyterian settler and displaced native Gael were living back to back and settlers, whether in South Africa or Ulster, are never a secure people. There is a distrust and fear of the neighbour. What the Plantation of the seventeenth century created were patterns of land ownership, patterns of distrust, suspicion, fear and sectarian attitudes and behaviour that have remained. Within Reformations that had, apart from the Anabaptists, failed to break the state-church or faith-politics merger, Presbyterians with an inherent strong suspicion of all centralised power, were themselves still highly political. They had come from a Scottish history of religio-political covenants. These were anti Catholic as well as anti Anglican. Centralised power was anathema to Presbyterians. Being highly political they believed strongly that the governing order should reflect the religious.[78] This also meant that religion could be heavily politicised and a settler psyche found it easy to politicise the Reformed theology of chosen people, promised land and covenant.

When their worst fears were realised in 1641 with the Catholic Rising, and when a Covenanting army led by General Monro arrived in 1642 to suppress the Catholic Rising, the officer class, all members of their Kirk Sessions in Scotland, quickly set about organising the disparate Ulster Scots into the first presbytery in Ulster. They did so in Carrickfergus and so the Presbyterian Church in Ireland was formally constituted, something that the General Assembly moved itself to Carrick for one day to commemorate in 1992. Now there was a Reformed Church organised around *"strict Old Testament social and religious codes its predestination defining who was saved and who was not. It was, in Akenson's words, 'a perfect tribal religion' for the Ulster Scots in their now promised land"*.[79] Of the three larger Protestant Churches in Ireland, Presbyterians would not only hold to fairly strict Calvinist theological and political models, they would hold to a more absolute belief in *sola scriptura*. Presbyterians do have a dissenting tradition and this was strongly evident in the theology and politics of the 1790s through the founding of the United Irishmen on the Cave Hill, Belfast, in 1791 and the 1798 Rising, especially their involvement in Antrim and Down.

An irony of Presbyterianism in Ireland is that the large exodus of Presbyterians in the years following 1708 to North America, became involved in a *'Brits out'* war on that continent. Meanwhile from about 1834 onwards the Ulster Scots in the north-east of Ireland became increasingly pro-Union with Britain and pro-Tory. They produced the Ulster Covenant and strongly resisted a Home Rule parliament for Ireland in 1912 and the years following. Presbyterianism is the largest Protestant Church in today's Northern Ireland and it took root in the region through politico-religious Articles of Plantation. The State of Northern Ireland after 1921 has given Presbyterians, along with other Protestants, a false sense of being a majority with power and entitlement. Yet on the island of Ireland, Protestantism remains a minority with an enduring sense of insecurity and their own form of victimhood. But then, is not Ireland a tragic tale of two historical victimhoods, one Catholic, the other Protestant, shaped by a religio-political sectarian past?

Methodists arrived in Ireland in the eighteenth century, not like the Anglicans and Presbyterians on the back of political invasion and intervention, but in the golden era of Protestant Ascendency. Methodists were the younger siblings of the Anglicans, their founder John Wesley an Anglican priest and living and dying an Anglican. He had no wish to found another Christian denomination but saw those who responded to his movement as Societies, gathering on Sunday evenings for the short preaching service and joining the *'great congregation'* of Anglicans on Sunday mornings for Holy Communion. Wesley visited Ireland twenty-one times and as preparation for his Irish visits he read accounts of the Catholic Rising of 1641. He believed these to be genuine accounts of the Irish massacre of 1641 and that more than two hundred thousand men, women and children were butchered within a few months. We now know that the numbers killed in 1641 numbered two thousand, mainly by drowning in the River Bann. The grossly exaggerated numbers were part of the propaganda that followed, which only in relatively recent years historical documentation has been able to put right. The massacres did, though, go deep into the Protestant psyche and John Wesley did repeatedly refer to them in his meticulous journals.

Wesley was of his time, and thought poorly of *'Papists'*. After visiting Castlebar he was surprised to *"find how little Irish Papists have changed in an hundred years".*[80] He thought they were as bitter and as blood thirsty as ever, and would freely cut a Protestants throat! But this was the height of the Protestant Ascendency with Catholics in possession of no more than 10% of land, and Penal Laws, though not always rigorously enforced, were still hanging over the Catholic majority. Whether John Wesley liked it or not, he and the Irish Methodists were seen as part of the Establishment, and when critical moments arose, such as the 1798 Rising, the Methodists were on the side of the Anglican Establishment, which is why they suffered during the Rising in Wexford.

Wesley did complain that the only way to convert Catholics was to impose Penal Laws, implying that there must be a better way. Yet he supported the Penal Laws, not to hurt Catholics, but to control them. In the Irish context he was to write a remarkable letter to a Roman Catholic, which expressed a tolerance beyond its time. Acknowledging that Catholics and Protestants did not agree on many things, nevertheless, he said, *"If your heart be as mine, give me your hand"*. Later Methodists defined themselves as *'friends of all and enemies of none'*, but this was often more mantra than reality. The Methodist Church was the first Protestant Church after the close-call and threat of the 1798 Rising to Protestant Ascendency, to set aside three Irish-speaking evangelists to convert Catholics to the true faith. Within a few years they were followed by the Anglicans and Presbyterians in what became known as the *'Second Reformation'*. But it was no more successful than the first. Protestants remained a minority and after 1829 Catholic confidence increased after Catholic Emancipation. As the Penal Laws were dismantled, the land issue came to the fore and as it began the process of being put right and justice done, not fully until 1906, the demand for, and resistance to, Home Rule dominated late nineteenth and early twentieth centuries. The gun came back to dominate Irish politics and God was invoked to support the Catholic-nationalist cause and the Protestant-unionist cause, presumably a Catholic god and a Protestant god! The Protestant churches were vehemently opposed to Home Rule, their church leaders among the first seven signatories of the Ulster Covenant, pledging *'to use any means necessary'* to defeat the Home Rule conspiracy. And by 1912 they knew that *'any means'* meant guns. The powerful Catholic Church was totally committed to Home Rule, which alone would represent the desires of the Irish people. But who were the Irish people? Catholics only?

In 1921 Ireland was partitioned, the culmination of at least four centuries of sectarian politics and religion. Partition did not create the problem of sectarianism. Sectarianism led to and created partition. The old sectarian scores were played again in Northern Ireland post-1969. They had never gone away and in religious and secular guises they remain. The Churches cannot wash their hands of sectarianism and five hundred years of Irish history. Not only in Ireland, but certainly in Ireland with deadly effect, the sectarianisation of Protestant and Catholic Reformations has shaped a terrible and violent history. But then on the European mainland the Reformations led to a thirty years war. The alignment of religion and politics with its human and structured lust for power and domination is nearly always violent and lethal. Sectarianism is a religio-political weapon of mass destruction. The Protestant and Catholic Reformations in Ireland created such a weapon. Any commemoration of Reformations in 2017 needs to be sober and robustly critical. In theological terms, repentance would go a long way!

9
The Reformations and Political Violence

One of the most difficult questions for any religion to answer is, why are religion and violence so often intimately connected? Or what makes violence religious in essence? Or why does religion so easily lend itself to violence? From earliest times war and religion have been deeply connected. Powers have invoked the gods or God and every superpower or empire in history has done so. It may be that when a power, an empire or a nation-state is asking people to go and kill and possibly be killed, it calls on the highest moral authority it knows, war gods or the warrior God, to legitimise, authorise or bless the violent cause. Every warring faction has claimed to have the sacred on its side. In part this is also the demonization of the other, the enemy. Those who lose their lives in warring or violent conflict are described in religious language, having made the supreme sacrifice, and there is no higher loyalty than laying down one's life for one's country. All of this is intended to give a religious veneer to war and violence. Memorialisation involves religious ritual or ritual with religious overtones. There is nothing new about Islamic State and its claiming of religion as a legitimising and motivating factor. Christianity has been setting the pace and model since the fourth century CE. Buddhism and Hinduism have had their religio-violent moments and Judaism, like Christianity, has had its texts of terror in the sacred writings. It is somewhat difficult to avoid the warrior God.

It is notoriously easy to simplify the religious dimension to violence or the violent dimension to religion. To simply say that religion causes violence is a kind of simplism. To claim that a violent conflict situation is not religious but political, as has been claimed in Northern Ireland and other regions, is equally simplistic. When looking at the sixteenth and seventeenth centuries and the violence and religious wars that took place, it is not possible to isolate religion as a sole source of anything. Society then was not like that. There was no separation between political, social, cultural, economic and religious dimensions to society. In our more secular time religion, we have imagined, belongs to the private side of life and has no role or is meant to have no role in public affairs. For a while this was true but the secularisation thesis has broken down and in the last forty years we have begun to realise that religion has not left the public stage. Many are now rethinking the role of religion in world affairs. Religion as isolated in the private sphere has proven to be something of a delusion. Islamic State is an example of religious extremism, but it cannot be understood apart from the political, social, cultural and economic dimensions. The challenge to all religion now is to clarify publicly what the essential ethics and values of religions are in a world of multi-dimensional realities. There is also the ultimate ethical challenge as to how power is used in the public sphere, be it religious, political, social, cultural or economic power, or the exercise and use of power across the multi-dimensional and integrated reality.

The era from 1550-1650 has been described as the *'age of religious wars'*. Ireland's religious wars continued right up to the end of the seventeenth century with the Williamite Wars. What happened in this era was not only about armies and battles. Because of deep religious divisions there were riots, persecutions, martyrdoms and witch-hunts. There was widespread carnage and we cannot take seriously the Reformations of the sixteenth century without being serious about the bloodshed they provoked. *"From the very start, the Protestant Reformation caused enormous social and political strife and outright bloodshed linked to religion"*.[81] Again the multiple and integrated dimensions of sixteenth century Europe or Christendom need to be noted. These religious wars included *"political contentions in which religion was the way by which conflicts in the commonwealths of state and Church were manifested"*.[82] At the heart of what erupted was Luther because at the Diet of Worms in 1521 he had defied not only the Pope but also the Holy Roman Emperor. Luther's challenge was to the religious and political world and both were threatened and challenged by what he had set in motion in Wittenberg 1517. His defiance at Worms turned Luther and his followers into outlaws. The Elector of Saxony, Frederick the Wise, had to rescue Luther and secretly carry him off to the safety of the Wartburg Castle. Luther was immediately in conflict with Emperor Charles V. All other princes or a city within the Holy Roman Empire supportive of Luther's reforms were now drawn into intense political conflict. To see the Reformations as merely religious is to fail to understand the nature of the sixteenth century European world and to misread them.

It was in Germany and Switzerland that violence first erupted. It took various forms, iconoclasm, persecutions, riots, massacres, wars and it was impossible to separate the spiritual and the secular, the religious and the worldly. While Luther was in hiding in the Wartburg, iconoclastic riots took place in Wittenburg, all of which was critical of Luther's leadership. Iconoclastic violence broke out in Switzerland with the utter destruction of images, relics and sacred vessels and all things considered idolatrous. All of this was not just about the destruction of property and things, it challenged the social and political order. It was ultimately about the abolition and end of the Catholic Church and in 1531 a battle took place in which Protestants and Catholics killed each other in the name of religion. The battle was a disaster for Protestants with several pastors dying in battle, the most high profile being the key Zurich reformer, Ulrich Zwingli. The Peace of Kappel was significant in that it led to the first legal recognition of the Protestant Churches by the Catholic authorities. Two very different churches could now exist within one nation. Though the peace was fragile, further bloodshed was avoided and Protestants and Catholics in some areas even managed to share the same buildings.

Germany and Switzerland, however now experienced another level of war or violence. Between 1524-1525 there erupted the Peasants War or Farmers War. At the heart of this war was not just religious rhetoric but a whole series of economic, political and social grievances.

The farmers appealed to the Gospel and Luther's assertion of freedom. Apocalyptic, religious language was evoked. Luther had defied the Church and the political order but he described the peasants as being involved in the *'devils work'*. The Peasants War has been described as one of *"the largest mass uprisings in the history of Europe before the French Revolution in 1789"*.[83] The old feudal system from medieval times was breaking down and was being replaced by the *"consolidation of power and centralisation of the early modern state, and as hard currency replaced exchange in kind as an ever-expanding economy"*.[84] There were growing bureaucracies and new taxes were levelled against the peasants. Where was justice and where was their place in the world? It was a time of radical change and there were political, economic and religious dynamics at work. Twelve Articles were drawn up but Luther had no time for them, publishing *'Against the Murderous and Thieving Hordes of Peasants'*. Luther defended the social order and the rights of the rulers. The Articles called for the abolition or readjustment of tithes, imposed by church or state. Also the abolition of serfdom, freedom to hunt and fish on landlords estates, a revaluation of all services done to feudal lords, an equitable and restructuring of rent assessments, the return of common fields seized by landlords and the abolition of the death tax. The peasants used violence as well as demanding a society conforming to the Word of God. They played Luther's *sola scriptura* card, much to his discomfort. But the landlords had greater power, and what is now called *'The Revolution of the Common Man' was brutally and violently crushed "in a sea of blood"*.[85]

In fairness Luther condemned both landlords and peasants, but he could not support the social reforms called for in the Twelve Articles. Luther had become a social conservative and supporter of the status quo. The article against serfdom he believed to be robbery, totally against the Gospel and if implemented, it would *"make all men (sic) equal, and turn the spiritual Kingdom of Christ into a worldly external kingdom"*.[86] There is a hint here of Luther's doctrine of two kingdoms, dualistic thinking which was destructive then and even more so in

Germany in the Nazi era.

A peace of sorts held for half a century, but there was always a war in the making. Religion and territory related to political power was a constant threat to any peace. Calvinists and Catholics were becoming increasingly aggressive and each made territorial gains. The opening of Jesuit schools threatened Protestants. Catholic and Protestant rulers formed new alliances. The war erupted in Bohemia, which, though ruled by the Catholic Hapsburgs, had effectively broken with Rome a century before Luther arrived on the scene. The war became known as the Thirty Years War lasting from 1618-1648. It was the largest and most destructive war of the early modern era. It was sparked when two representatives of the Holy Roman Emperor were thrown out of a window of the Hradčany Castle in Prague. The war was now between Catholic Emperor Ferdinand and the Calvinist Frederick, head of the Protestant Union. This was a religio-political and territorial war! *"While there is no denying that religion was a catalyst and a constant factor in the war, political issues were also increasingly significant"*.[87] At the heart of it all was Hapsburg power, wanting to maintain power and domination, with the Protestant princes equally determined to resist. It was a bloody war and like many wars was driven by fear.

> *Almost all the combatants were activated by fear rather than lust of conquest or passion of faith. They wanted peace and they fought for thirty years to be sure of it. They did not learn then, and have not learned since, that war only breeds war.*[88]

Religion by itself does not cause war or violence. It is when it is aligned with political power and where territory, land and fear are involved that religion becomes a potent factor in war and violence. And with politics it often fails to learn that war is self-perpetuating, war breeds war and it becomes extremely difficult to break out of the spiral of killing and violence.

It was a long, brutal and messy war, involving much of Europe. It *"was the first modern military conflict to involve so many nations and to affect civilian populations directly, as enormous armies moved across the landscape without sufficient provisions…".*[89] Whilst not in one sense a religious war, religion was so much bound up with it that, it was a consequence of the Protestant Reformation. The effect of the war, though, was to ensure that religion was no longer a major source of conflict and violence in Europe. Whilst not a major source of WW1, religion was invoked by all sides in that catastrophic conflict. Religions still have major moral questions and challenges in relation to war and violence.

The Thirty Years War came to an end with the Treaty of Westphalia or the Peace of Westphalia. The final signatures were made on 24 October 1648. It was a significant Treaty. It set:

> *…the ground plan of the international order in central Europe for the next century and more. It registered both the ascendancy of France and the subordination of the Habsburgs to the German princes. On the religious issue, it ended the strife in Germany by granting the same rights to Calvinists as to Catholics and Lutherans.*[90]

A way of solving confessional disputes through negotiation was agreed and the Treaty did bring an era of politico-religious contentions in Germany to an end. But it was not a European peace accord as France and Spain continued their war. The Peace of Westphalia set the religious lines of modern European states.

Whilst not caused by the Reformations, the massive witch hunts of Europe involved both Protestants and Catholics. The extermination of witches was one thing Protestants and Catholics agreed on. The witch craze lasted from the 15th to the 18th centuries, when suspected witches were burned, hanged or tortured by the thousands. It was an era of paranoia and hysteria and non-conformism meant certain death. It has never been possible to precisely define a witch, but in the context of the European witch craze, many of the women put to death (and the majority were women) appear to be little more than practitioners of alternative medicine, practitioners of old cures. But they were perceived as interfering with nature. *"In Wiesensteig, in south-west Germany, 63 women were executed as witches between 1562 and 1563 for causing a violent hailstorm".*[91]

The Catholic Prince Bishop of Bamberg had a purpose-built witch house with torture chamber and biblical texts. Between 1623-1633 he is reputed to have burned six hundred witches. Europe's leading witch hunter was a Protestant professor at Leipzig, Dr Benedikt Carpzov, who published a book on conducting witch trials. He apparently had read the Bible fifty three times and was a weekly communicant, who is reputed to have brought about the deaths of some 20,000 witches.[92]

One of the most famous witch hunters in history was James I, who was King of England from 1603 to 1625. His personal crusade resulted in the deaths of thousands of women in Scotland, his native land, and hundreds more south of the border.[93]

In Scotland, especially, James encouraged and sanctioned savage torture of witches as a means of getting confessions. In 1597 James published his *Demonologie* in Scotland. James was an ardent witch-hunter, a learned person of faith who also gave the English-speaking world the King James Bible in 1611. In the same year as his publication on Demonologie, only fourteen years earlier than KJV Bible, some four hundred suspected witches were tried in Scotland and about half of them executed. It is estimated that during the Reformation some 1500 witches were killed in Scotland.

It is puzzling that the era of the Reformations saw Catholic and Protestant combine to persecute and execute mainly women as suspected witches and agents of the Devil. It is difficult not to conclude that the paranoia and mass hysteria, which gripped different parts of Europe, was deeply misogynistic. And religion cannot be dissociated from the misogyny or deeply religious individuals from leading roles in stirring the witch craze. From the 1550s, orthodoxy, confessionalism and social disciplining were prominent factors. In that era the persecution of witches increased and intensified. Toleration was not a virtue even though Luther had introduced the word to the German language. But Luther had only introduced the word to dismiss it. He said *"Faith suffers nothing and the Word tolerates nothing"*. What Luther meant was that the Word of God allowed no compromises.[94] This meant that one had to be absolutely certain that one had the Word of God and its clear meaning. Could Luther or anyone else be so sure? There could therefore be no toleration of other confessions or religions and no toleration of demonic forces or witchcraft. Misogyny, hatred of others, war, killing and patriarchy, violence to achieve or defend power and territory, were all permissible to religion, presumably sanctioned by the Word of God!

10
Sola Scriptura: Scripture Alone?

At the heart of the Protestant Reformations is the affirmation *Sola Scriptura*, Scripture Alone. When Martin Luther nailed his theses to the church door in Wittenberg, he was calling for a public debate. At one level Luther was opposing the theologically false and socially unjust practice of indulgences. There was nothing about indulgences that was biblical as far as Luther was concerned. The touchstone for Luther was the Bible and the necessary reform of the church was about recovering biblical models and practice. Indulgences were the issue of the moment but there was much else about the church that was distorted and was unbiblical. At a deeper level Luther was raising the question of authority. Where does authority lie in the church and for the church? As a professor in Wittenberg, lecturing to his students on Psalms and Romans especially, had brought him on a journey. Luther was a troubled monk burdened by the medieval theology of his time and by his image of God frozen in his experience of his own strict and judgemental father. In the Bible Luther was discovering liberating truth. Indulgences were the antitheses of all the enlightenment. Authority lay in something much more radical and liberating than the Pope or the traditions of the church. The liberating word was in scripture. So Luther concludes with *sola scriptura*. The Bible was the only authoritative standard and the only rule for faith, practice and church. *Sola scriptura* became his key battle cry against the Church and for reform. It is not possible to understand Luther and the Protestant Reformations without noting *sola scriptura*.

What this meant for Luther was that all theology, piety and practice had to conform to the teaching of the Bible. Anything that Luther felt to be unbiblical was rejected. Only a biblical way of thinking faith, practicing faith and being church was acceptable. Other protestant reformers took up this battle cry. In Zurich, Ulrich Zwingli was defying food laws. He wasn't the first to do so in Zurich. On the first Friday of Lent 1522, a group of Zurich laypersons met to eat sausages in defiance of the abstention from meat requirement, and did so with a lot of public fanfare. Sausages became a test case with Zwingli insisting that all laws be judged by scripture. In the end the civil authorities ruled on all the sausage eaters on the basis of *sola scriptura*. Having won the sausage battle, Zwingli and others began to question other beliefs and practices on biblical grounds.

The radical reformers or the left wing of the Reformations, were also appealing to *sola scriptura*. The problem for the classical reformers was that the left wing did not think them radical enough. On biblical grounds they went further as they sought to get back to the early church in all its apostolic purity. The Christendom church was fallen, infant baptism was the sign of this fallen church aligned with the state and its wars. Non-violence was the apostolic way for a purely voluntary community of believers. They too were appealing to sola scriptura and they too were interpreting scripture as the basis of their model of faith and practice. But this was a problem for the principle of sola scriptura. *"In many ways, their literal interpretation of the Bible, and especially the New Testament, followed the reforming principle of sola scriptura to logical conclusions that neither Zwingli nor Luther were willing to accept".*[95] Which of the Reformation models was biblically based?

Meanwhile the farmers had revolted and the bloody Peasants War was fought from 1524-1525. At the end, the Twelve Articles were produced by the peasants. They appealed to the Bible as the highest authority of all, believed that the legality of all their demands were to be judged by the Bible alone. All their demands, essentially for justice, the farmers were convinced were *"contained in God's word"*. Furthermore, their interpretation of scripture was beyond questioning… *"the rebels naively offered up this very Lutheran sola scriptura article as their trump card".*[96]

Luther, who believed absolutely in *sola scriptura*, had described the peasants as doing the devils' work and their demand for equality as robbery and turning the Kingdom of Christ into a secular kingdom. Who was right and if ultimate authority lay in the Bible alone, then whose interpretation of the biblical text was authoritative and why?

The Council of Trent met from 1545-1563 and produced the Catholic Reformation. At its first session from December 1545 to March 1547, the Council addressed theology and the first decrees it issued were on Scripture and both were directed against Protestant claims. The first was addressed directly to *sola scriptura*. Trent affirmed that the church had authority to interpret scripture and there was the role of tradition, the accumulated teaching and wisdom of the church through the ages. The decree also firmly established the canonical authority and legitimacy of the apocryphal books that Protestants had excluded from their authoritative canon. These were books such as Tobit and Macabees. The second decree pronounced the Latin Vulgate Bible translation to be error free, a kind of biblical infallibility.

The problem with polemics is that protagonists define themselves in sharp opposites. Statements are less affirmative than defensive and language is used in absolute and oppositional ways than a calmer environment would require or allow. For the next four and more centuries the simplistic understanding of Protestant-Catholic tensions and self-identities has been Scripture or Tradition, either-or. Despite the fact that both Luther and Calvin did not really think the faithful could read and interpret scripture for themselves, and each produced Confessions and Institutes to show the faithful how to interpret, Protestants have never quite worked out the tension and relationship between scripture and tradition. Luther and Calvin set out immediately to create tradition and then attempted to show their followers how to interpret the Bible, some might say, to control the interpretation of the Bible. This in turn began to shape Protestant tradition. Protestantism, in all its varieties, believes more than it thinks, in tradition and the role of tradition. Calvin's Institutes, Luther's Catechism, Anglican Articles, Westminster Confession of Faith and Wesley's *Notes on the New Testament*, however much they may be described by Presbyterians of the Confession, as a *'subordinate standard'*, have become tradition, shaping the respective interpretations of the Bible and theological doctrines.

> *Roman Catholics believe, more fervently than Protestants imagine, that Scripture and tradition are complimentary rather than antithetical sources of truth. And Protestants sola scriptura does not mean that the Holy Spirit ceased to be active when the New Testament canon was complete, but rather that through the New Testament canon he (sic) continues to be radically active in the church, both in judgement and renewal.*[97]

Sola scriptura has been more complex than has been imagined. The complexity and problem was evident within the first generation of the Reformations. Classical reformers, radical reformers and the farmers in revolt were coming up with very different interpretations of the Bible whilst all affirming scripture alone. But which interpretation of scripture was truly biblical, if any? And with Trent declaring the Vulgate translation of the Bible error free, where did that leave Luther's translation into German and later the King James translation into English? Was any translation error free or in any way infallible? This is not only a question of interpretation or version, but a question of authority. Where does authority lie? And the issues have become more acute since the nineteenth century unearthing of multiple manuscripts of biblical texts, providing unprecedented sources and earlier ones, for translation. Not surprisingly this has led to a plethora of translations in various languages, more than ever. The globalisation of faith and the rise of different models of contextualised theology have led to diversity of interpretative approaches to scripture. It is possible to identify at least fourteen different models of biblical interpretation.[98] If Luther was really claiming that he had the only true interpretation of scripture, it proved not to be possible then and is impossible now.

Faith communities still make absolute claims to biblical truth. The position taken on *'traditional'* marriage is claimed, usually without substantiation, to be the biblical teaching on marriage. Or the stance taken on gays and lesbians or transgendered people claim to be faithful to the Bible. Or that male and female are complimentary is pronounced biblical. Or women in priesthood or ministry is neither biblical nor in the tradition. Protestant conservatives often argue against gay marriage, not only on biblical grounds, but also on the basis of tradition. Traditionally the church supported slavery on biblical grounds. The Dutch Reformed Church in South Africa believed that the system of apartheid had a biblical basis. Wars have been backed with appeal to scripture and remembrance and memorial services in relation to war use scripture, especially John's Gospel, *'greater love hath no man…'* But can we be so absolute, certain and sure that our interpretation of scripture is true and authoritative?

Two realities ensure difficulties. No one reads the Bible without denominational or theological presuppositions. There is no presuppositionless interpretation. As fallible and finite humans it is important to read the Bible without bias. Lutherans read the Bible through the lens of justification by faith, but is that enough? Presbyterians read through the lens of the sovereignty of God or covenant. Catholics read from the perspective of the magisterium. Methodist reading is shaped by the eighteenth century lens of John Wesley. This is not to disparage tradition. It has much to teach but it too was not without presuppositions or free from bias. Interpretation then or now is also through contemporary lens. Interpretation is contextual. The rich and poor read the Bible differently. The farmers did in the sixteenth century. Latin American and North Americans read the same text differently. European women and African women will have different interpretative approaches to a book like Ruth in the Hebrew Bible. To risk a stereotype, Protestants and Catholics in Northern Ireland may read the same scripture, even the same lectionary on Sundays, but interpret the biblical vision of justice differently. The late Ian Paisley and Desmond Tutu read the Exodus story in the Hebrew Bible as though there were two different Bibles. All Christians of whatever denomination or tradition claim the authority of the Bible. But the authority of the Bible and the authority of our interpretations of the Bible are never the same. Despite what some fundamentalists claim that the Bible says, it never just says, it is always an interpretation and an interpretation with presupposition and bias.

All Christian traditions claim the Bible as their primary source or their foundational documents. Vatican II was very clear on the primacy of scripture for Catholics. Some Protestants claim inerrancy and infallibility. Prior to Vatican II the Catholic Church would have made a similar claim. Trent claimed the Vulgate was without error, but claims to be without error, infallible or inerrant go far beyond anything the Bible claims for itself. There was no agreement about *sola scriptura* at the Reformations. Different interpretations occurred.

If *sola scriptura* means anything, it means that the Bible is the primary source document for faith and practice. There is no mono-interpretation. There is interpretative dispute as there is interpretative dispute over a number of issues within the Bible itself. There is light, truth and the word of God to be encountered, but how do we arrive at what can only be provisional truth? How can we know what is approximately true for life?

Anglicans and Methodists have believed that they need to go beyond *sola scriptura*, that by itself it's not enough. What emerged in their processes of reflection and faithful living became known as the Quadrilateral. For Anglicans it began with holding to a solid biblical foundation that prevented or controlled the misuse of scripture and private interpretations. The misuse of scripture has always been part of history. Anglicans looked to the primitive church, from the first centuries of Christian history. They looked to these early traditions and theologians so long as they followed scripture as their primary authority. Scripture had a normative authority and there was something authoritative about the primitive church as it interpreted its narrative authority the Bible. There was also the use of reason and reason was a partner in theological conversation. Human reason is used to discern and critically evaluate and reflect. Life is experiential. We experience light, truth, and love. Experience is part of our engagement with life, personally and collectively.

The Quadrilateral of scripture, tradition, reason and experience was an interdependent framework through which light, truth and faith could be searched for and found. None of the four is sola and none in itself, and even together for that matter, infallible. John Wesley, founder of Methodism did his theological reflection through the Quadrilateral lens.

> *We begin with the rule of Scripture, for it is primary. Tradition (the early centuries being privileged) instructs the church, especially regarding the doctrinal interpretation of the Bible. Reason, individually but especially, collectively, elucidates God's way of being active in the created order. And experience, especially as religion experienced in celebration and worship brings to life in the heart and mind of the believer the saving work of God in Christ.*[99]

It is within the parameters of this Quadrilateral dynamic that theological reflection is done and people of faith begin to define afresh, and again and again, where they are going in the world. It can help to avoid the misuse and abuse of the Bible, avoid bibliolatry, faith in a book before faith in the mystery of the divine disclosed in the living Word, Christ. It also helps to interpret the Bible with humility, knowing that no interpretation is the last word. So the Book of Discipline of the United Methodist Church:

> *Wesley believed that the living core of the Christian faith was revealed in Scripture, illuminated by tradition, vivified in personal experience, and confirmed by reason.*[100]

Sola scriptura needs, and has, partners.

11
Legacies and Living Beyond Sixteenth Century Questions

Every age and generation has got to deal with its own questions and shape living faith in its own time, place and context. There is no timeless Christian faith and a study of the history of Christianity shows that there never has been. The world keeps changing and the articulation and practice of faith changes in response and through engagement. The modern history of Ireland has produced a conservative Catholicism and Protestantism, reluctant to change theology and practice. Perhaps being a relatively small island with a modern history of conflict and violence has shaped a conservative and at times ultra conservative faith. The Reformations left in Ireland a legacy, five centuries of history, deeply polarised with divisions that run deep. In 1979 it was not possible for the Pope to come to Northern Ireland and even though Protestant Church leadership met Pope John Paul II in Dublin, it was for some and in part about protest. That Pope Francis will be welcomed in Northern Ireland by all of the Protestant Churches and unionist political leadership is a huge step, which shows how far we have moved in thirty-eight years. Yet the past remains a burden and not a few, in terms of religion and politics, seem at home there. But just as the decade of centenaries, 1912-1922, has reminded us that the questions and issues of then are not those of now, because the world has changed and the questions have changed, so the sixteenth century is definitely not the twenty-first century. However the Reformations will be commemorated in 2017, we cannot allow the present to be hedged about by sixteenth century questions. If the questions of then define now, then commemoration and holding onto a sixteenth century worldview will become a way of avoiding the hard and challenging questions of a very different world and time. Commemoration needs to be future orientated and become a springboard to wrestle with twenty-first century questions, the big public and global questions, and shape faith, ethics and practice for the only world we have.

This does not mean dismissing the past, casting the Protestant and Catholic Reformations into the dustbin. There are positive legacies, insightful discoveries as well as negative and destructive legacies about which we need to be critical and from which we can learn. There are always things that could and should have been done differently, though much of this is hindsight. And there are always complex forces at play, then as now, that are more powerful than the personalities and dynamics of reformers.

Luther's spiritual quest was for a gracious God. He was of Christendom and believed that religion, politics, culture and economics could not be separated. He was not only a child of Augustinian theology with its dark pessimism about human nature, he was also a child of the Renaissance with its emphasis on individualism. His own theological tradition oppressed him, his image of God shaped by his strict, judgemental father and upbringing, all troubled him as an individual and trapped him in what later became known as the introverted conscience of the West. God was a stern judge, a moralistic and condemning Father. Was that all, or was there a gracious God, loving, compassionate and forgiving?

Bad childhood experiences and upbringing can be oppressive and destructive for many. Physical and sexual abuse is even more destructive of people. Moralistic Church teaching and violent God-images trap people in fear and encourage violent attitudes and behaviours. Atheism for some is a real moral choice, not only in response to childhood experiences and to moralistic and oppressive church teaching, it is for many a moral choice in the face of the terrible suffering of humans and the planet. Luther's quest for a gracious God has a contemporary resonance. At the heart of life and the universe is there a gracious, compassionate, loving energy, power or presence? Whatever sacredness or transcendence there is, is the essence gracious, loving and compassionate? Or is there just a cold, brutal nothingness? Luther did discover a sense of the sacred, the Other or God who was gracious, unconditionally accepting, loving and liberating. Luther experienced this as a gift, gracious unconditionality that set him free from the moralism of *'must do'* and achieving the impossible. On that he could now trust or wager his life.

What was experienced as the liberating and life-shaping response to his struggle and quest, he described theologically as justification by faith. It became the key lens by which he read and interpreted the Bible, his master text being Romans 5. In time it became the defining essence of the Lutheran Church and for over four hundred years a battle ground between Protestants and Catholics. The last quarter of the twentieth century saw dialogue rather than polemic, and substantial agreement was reached on justification by faith by Protestants and Catholics. The only surprise now is that it took over four hundred years to reach common ground. But this was agreement and common ground on doctrine, theological formulation. Meanwhile, thousands of Protestants and Catholics had experienced a gracious God, a loving sacred at the heart of life, outside of doctrinal formulation. There were also thousands of Protestants and Catholics who struggled with destructive and oppressive life experiences and of moralistic and oppressive church teaching and who never found a gracious God. And that included many who claimed to be orthodox believers and that their doctrine of justification by faith was alone true.

Luther's quest and experience remain as authentic to the twenty-first century, but he missed something crucial in his reading of Romans and even misread Paul. This bombshell was dropped in 1960 by Lutheran Bishop Krister Stendahl. If anyone was going to question Luther and over four hundred years of Lutheran history, it had to be a Lutheran bishop! Stendahl drew critical attention to the introspective conscience of the West. This was a critique of individualism and the narrowly introspective Augustinian and Lutheran interpretation of Paul, which focused on individual salvation and justification. Luther's reading of Romans had created a dichotomy between grace and law, faith and works which had the destructive consequence of setting Christianity over against Judaism and contributing to anti-Semitism, of the kind which had led to the twentieth century Holocaust in Luther's Germany. But Luther had misread law as legalism, when the Hebrew Torah was life-giving teaching at the heart of ancient Israel's tradition. *"Stendahl was dismantling an entire interpretative framework, one built on bad anthropology and a serious misunderstanding of Jewish Torah. He was also exposing a fundamental Western assumption that religion was separate from politico-economic life"*.[101] This would now require a more contextual and historical reading of Paul and this has been true of studies of Paul since then.

Paul was not a Lutheran or a Protestant, but a Jew and his language and thought forms cannot be understood apart from his Jewish tradition. Furthermore Paul was not a Protestant writing Romans in opposition to Roman Catholics. He wrote all of his letters in the shadow of the Roman empire and far from criticising Judaism, as Luther thought, Paul was challenging and critiquing Roman imperialism. If we want to better understand Paul and justification by faith then: *"get Paul and his letter to the Romans out of the sixteenth century polemical Reformation world and back into the first-century imperial Roman world"*.[102]

Reading Paul the Jew within the historical context of the Roman empire, recovers a crucial dimension to justification that Luther completely missed. Justification is closely associated with and inseparable from the key Jewish vision of justice. Justification is justice. Paul was not being religious in the sense of individualistic and introverted conscience and soul. He was being radically political and given his Jewish background and historical context, Romans is to be read as a theo-political document. Paul is critiquing human social and political injustice. It is a comprehensive indictment of his world and his critique is related to divine impartiality (Romans 2 v 12-16). God requires justice and Paul's claim is that *"the true basis for justice, for just societies and a just world, is to be found in the messianic announcement to which he and his readers seek to be faithful".*[103] The empire's claim to justice is false. Pax Romana was based on force and violence. God's way of creating justice and relationships based on justice (righteousness) and peace or total wellbeing has been disclosed in the life, teachings and praxis of Jesus. Peace only comes through justice, social, economic and political justice and right relations rooted in such justice. Had Luther made the connection between justification and socio-political justice as in Paul's Hebrew/Jewish tradition, he might not have been so anti-Jewish and more importantly, he might have responded differently to the sixteenth century farmers in revolt. As for a twenty-first century Irish context and Paul's justification by faith:

> *There will be no overcoming sectarianism in Northern Ireland without justice for all in public life. This will mean putting justice at the heart of the educational system, at the heart of our political arrangements of power and our economic, banking and commercial systems. It will mean a health system based on justice as well as a police service and criminal justice system. The politico-ethical message of Romans is that without justice there is no reconciliation, peace and desired future. Unless we get the practice of justice right, there will be no shared future.*[104]

The Protestant Reformations left a legacy of spiritual equality that was radically social and political in its implications. This was expressed in the idea of the priesthood of all believers. One of the most widespread distortions of this affirmation is that Catholics need a priest to mediate between themselves and God. Protestants are their own priests and don't need anyone else. It is a Protestant misunderstanding and distortion and has been widely held within Irish Protestantism. It is both an individualistic and sectarian distortion. Having said that, the reformers were less than precise in how they expressed and interpreted this affirmation.

Rather than an individualistic idea, it had to do with a community.

The Protestant reformers highlighted the High Priesthood of Christ, the priestly go-between between God and humans. The flip side of this was that Jesus was God's representative to humankind. Jesus was the bridge between the divine and the human. Or Jesus was the window through which the graciousness and love of the sacred could be recognised and experienced. John's Gospel described Jesus as *'the Word made flesh'*, the reason, mind and purpose of God disclosed through a human life. The same Gospel also affirmed that Jesus was *"the lamb of God who takes away the sins of the world"* (John 1 v 29). Jesus is the high priest and suffering servant who offers himself in love to disclose the liberating love at the heart of the universe to struggling humankind. Those who in faith stake their lives on this priestly representative, and his suffering love become a community of priests, or what I Peter describes a *'royal priesthood'*, a community offering sacrifices of worship and loving service on behalf of the world (I Peter 2 v 5). Their active role as a community is to make known to the larger community of humanity, and indeed all creation, the light, graciousness, love, compassion, mercy, justice and peace of the divine. Whatever functional distinctions are made between clergy and laity, all are priests in sacrificial service to the world through light, truth, love, justice and peace. All are equally covenant people, actively committed to neighbourliness and the common good.

Religion by its very nature is not a private matter. The secularisation thesis deluded itself that it was, which is why religion, and not just Christianity has not left the public square.

Because religion is intrinsically social and cultural, it informs and shapes a peoples' moral behaviour as profoundly or as negligibly, as it does their spiritual belief. Religious doctrine and liturgy are propositions: they become reality only as people apply them to their everyday lives.[105]

The priesthood of all believers did not stay in the church or only revolutionise the church. By its social and cultural power it shaped and revolutionised German society. The Protestant Reformations left an indelible moral imprint on German society that spread beyond Germany, even though Protestantism did not become the majority religion of Europeans, and even less of the rest of the world. The moral power of spiritual equality shaped a moral imprint that translated into social and political equality.

Worship and liturgy are public and political acts, often subversive and a radical act of re-describing and reimagining the world. What happened to the old abbey on the Scottish island of Iona is a parable of the social and political power of the spiritual. In the Middle Ages the abbey had a chancel and a nave. A screen separated them from each other. Then the Reformations happened and Iona abbey became a ruin. Under the leadership of George MacLeod, a Church of Scotland minister, the abbey was restored, but significantly, without the screen. Today in Iona, all sit and worship together without distinction, a community of priests, spiritually equal.[106] The primary emphasis and key activity of the Iona community is social and political justice. The spiritual equality legacy of the Reformations, still needs radical working out through worship and action and sacrificial service in today's unequal world.

12
Radical Reformations Now

Just how radical were the Reformations and did they mark the birth of a revolution? Steven Ozmet draws attention to three different narratives. One narrative is that the Reformations tell the story of the division of Western Christendom and the loss of religious unity, probably forever. The fragmentation and denominationatising of Western Christianity continues today. The second narrative is of the Reformations awakening German nationalism and the shaping of German culture and character. Germany's role in Europe and place within Western nations is an ongoing debate. The third narrative is that the Reformations marked a spiritual revolution, which drove society and politics, but did more than that. It *makes injustice and bondage within the inner life as portentous as those which afflict peoples physical lives. For people living then, the struggle against sin and death, and the devil became as basic as that for bread, land and self-determination*.[107]

The latter narrative, perhaps, points to the inseparability of the inner and outer struggles. The struggle against sin and death is also the struggle for bread and land. The inner and the outer are not easily separated and in what happened in the sixteenth century Reformations they were not separated. Spiritual revolution can be social and political revolution. This is not always the case because there are forms of spirituality and piety, and renewal associated with them, that are escapist and otherworldly. The Reformations, whatever else they were, were not so spiritual as to be divorced from socio-political and economic realities. They did ignite a conflagration, but we still struggle to understand them or even why they left a sectarian legacy as in Ireland.

The Catholic Reformation has often been overlooked, certainly by Protestants. Protestantism did not take hold of southern Europe, but spread north. Though Christendom was divided and in a sense destroyed, the Catholic Church remained a significant institution, and numerically greater. The reforms at Trent did set the culture of the Church for centuries. Vatican I did not change Trent but made the power and identity of the papacy more absolute. It was Vatican II in the early 1960s that introduced radical reforms, the oft quoted *'gale'* that Pope John XXIII allowed to blow through his open windows. Some feel that the next three Popes rowed back on these reforms, others that they will take a considerable time to implement. After all, the Church works within a more divine timespan than earthly! Or is that a useful excuse? Others now see Pope Francis as a model of liberating hope for a renewing and renewed Church.

Perhaps the most significant consequence of the Catholic Reformation was the missionary expansion. This had already begun before Luther, but mission at home, and in territories beyond Europe, were impacted by the Catholic Reformation. The expansion into South America and Asia was significant, even though it meant an unholy alliance between missionaries, colonists and empire builders. This was not a feature of Protestantism in its first century, but therein after it too spread to Africa and Asia on the back of imperialism. The Catholic expansionism was seen as providential, *"perhaps even as predestined, or as a divine counterbalancing act, as God's response to the Protestant revolt in Europe."*[108]

If the Protestant Reformations created a new paradigm of faith and theology, and became a world force, as Hans Küng believes, then the driving force was not Luther but John Calvin. On the 27 May 1564 when Calvin died from physical exhaustion and serious illness, such crowds gathered in Geneva to mourn and respect his body lying in state, that worried officials brought forward his burial. They feared the making of a new saint![109] Calvin is the one believed to have made Protestantism a world power. Outside Germany and Scandinavia, Calvin drove Protestantism. Luther remained a provincial German. But even though the later Geneva memorial put Calvin at the centre and left out Luther, *"There would have been no Calvin, without Luther."*[110]

Luther was the prime mover in a theological revolution, what Küng likens to a *"Copernican shift in theology: away from the all too human ecclesiocentricity of a powerful church to the christocentricity of the gospel, all under the sign of the freedom of the Christian…"* [111] The heart of things was no longer the powerful institution of the church, but the liberating power of Christ. Germany had been under the papal thumb with political, social and cultural life dominated by the church. The decentring of the church and, as Luther saw it, the recentering of Christ, was the radical liberation of religious, social, political and cultural life. This was why German princes and rulers threw their lot in with the Protestant Reformation. All of life was liberated and set free from personal and collective tyranny. There is a massive clue here as to why theology in its thought forms, concepts, articulation and practice changes. Societal or social crisis brings about radical theological change, or a paradigm shift. When there is a radical crisis there is the beginning of radical change. *"Luther's theology was first of all a theology of crisis."* [112]

For over three decades Ireland, and in particular Northern Ireland, endured political violence and bloodshed. During this time the churches went into decline numerically and in the domination of public power, but still no radical shift in theology has taken place. There are signs of retreat behind familiar barricades and a fearful siege mentality or victimhood (faith is under attack and freedoms destroyed), but no paradigm shift in theology, no creative theological response to crises. Brexit, the American Presidential election, the rise of ethno-nationalism and far-right politics are probably the sign or symptoms of the West in decline and the end of a Western and European hegemon. The fear, anxiety and insecurity that underpins this and the growing instability of the world, is a crisis moment that calls for a radical shift in theology. The old models of faith, Protestant and Catholic, will not do. We cannot live with sixteenth century questions and relive sixteenth century battles. Christian faith in the West needs a radical, paradigm shift, a radical and robust theological response to a crisis, a new theology of crisis.

From the Reformations came the Protestant Principle. It was articulated by twentieth century Protestant theologian Paul Tillich. Tillich did not invent the Principle, but gave articulation to what had been at the heart of Protestantism. He defined it as *"the divine and human protest against any absolute claim made for a relative reality, even if this claim is made by the Protestant church. The Protestant principle is the gauge of every religious and cultural reality, including the religion and culture which calls itself Protestant."* [113] At the heart of the Protestant Reformations was the first Word from Sinai, *"You shall have no other gods before me"* (Exodus 20 v 3). No partial object of loyalty can become an ultimate object of loyalty, including the Bible and Protestantism. The Protestant Principle means that loyalty to nation, country or state cannot become ultimate either as it did in the nineteenth and twentieth centuries with destructive and catastrophic consequences, and as threatens to do so again in Europe and the US. When loyalty to Protestantism or Catholicism becomes ultimate and uncritical loyalty, the Protestant Principle calls such loyalty into question. No nation-state's interests and no church interests are to be identified with God's will. The Protestant Principle calls into question the divine right of kings (it didn't when James I invented the divine right doctrine), the divine right of empire, superpower or state (it hasn't really for the last century of American power and domination). Catholic theologian Gabriel Daly points up the irony of the Principle to both Protestantism and Catholicism.

There is some irony in the thought that biblical fundamentalism offends against the spirit of Protestantism, which claims to recognise that the sovereignty of God cannot be restricted by external circumstances like the creation of a book. There is equal irony in the thought that the institutional fundamentalism of papal government can offend against the spirit of genuine Catholicism, which is not sectarian and aims at universal validity.[114]

The Protestant Principle does not belong exclusively or apply solely to Protestantism. It is a shared Principle raising critical questions against any attempt to give ultimacy and ultimate loyalty to church institution, theological system, state, nation, political or economic system or cultural identity. It has never featured much in the modern history of Ireland, ecclesiastical or political. It might even be said that in Northern Ireland, what was once described as *"a Protestant state for Protestant people"*, no one really believed in the Protestant Principle!

It may be that the most radical affirmation to emerge from the Protestant Reformations was, in Latin, *Ecclesia Reformata Sed Semper Reformanda*, the church reformed always to be reformed. In a sense it is the logical extension of the Protestant Principle. Anything, including the church, Bible or nation, can become an idol, a substitute loyalty for God, who can never be found too easily, where incomprehensible mystery is forever beyond our experience, conceptualisation or definition. The Protestant Principle stands against the domestication of God and will not allow us to ever think that we have arrived at some finally realised truth that frees us from further questioning, questing and searching. The church in its theological beliefs, organisational structures and moral systems can never arrive either. Nothing is static, everything changes and changes often, if it is to be alive, vibrant, truly a body of pilgrim people on a never-ending journey. Within the biblical narrative, the greatest and constant temptation was to the sin of idolatry. The German Confessional Church opposed the idolatry of nationalism in its Barmen Declaration of 1934. At its heart the resistance was *'Christ is Lord, not Hitler'*. Other events and powers, such as Hitler, Nazism and anti-Semitism were to be resisted and repudiated. Sadly, the majority of German Christians did not stand with Barmen. The most insidious idolatry the church faces is the idolatry within. German-American theologian Reinhold Niebuhr saw the critical point. *"We must fight their falsehood with our truth, we must fight the falsehood in our truth"*.[115] It is the possibility of the falsehood in our truth, no less when claims are made to be *'Bible-believing Christians'* or a *'Bible-believing church'*, or *"the one true church outside of which there is no salvation"* (not the monopoly of any one tradition), that calls for critical awareness and critical self-judgement on our religious traditions and demands semper reformanda, reformed always to be reformed. Reformation is continuous, on-going, and is called for especially in critical moments of history in church or societal life.

> *The Reformation was not completed in the sixteenth century: it is never completed. We may for the sake of comfort try to transform Protestantism into a closed system; but it breaks out again. It has no 'infallible' voice to silence other voices in decrees that are 'irreformable'. Protestantism cannot be static.*[116]

The above is a Protestant-limited statement, pertinent and insightful nonetheless. Vatican Council II emphasised on-going reform. Pope John XXIII in calling the Council, used an Italian word, *aggieornamento*, which means updating, and became the guiding principle of Vatican II. From the fifteenth century the Catholic Church had followed the principle that *"men (sic) must be changed by religion, not religion by men"*. But John was looking in the opposite direction. *"Aggieornamento meant the church had to change to meet the needs of the times, that is the changes taking place outside itself…it was… rather a disengagement from the limitations of the past and from a culture no longer viable"*.[117] Reform was a focus and outcome summarised as: *"Instead of regarding itself as spotless and all holy, the church must acknowledge its errors, failings, and sins and continually reform itself"*.[118]

Always to be reformed is a shared emphasis of Protestants and Catholics, though how open to continuous reform Protestant and Catholic traditions are, is a matter of critical judgement. What happened in the sixteenth century was not the end of Reformation and was never meant to be. Theologically, the Holy Spirit did not come alive again in the 1500s and then withdraw from the church and the world. The church cannot be renewed once but is open to a life of constant renewal. The church should expect to be shaken, judged, purged and remade, not once, but often, as often as it falls into its own idolatry and continues to be a community of sinners, very fallible people. It has been prone to forget or even deny the latter and finalise and totalise its theology and practice. It even happened to the Protestant Reformations; everything became consolidated and settled into a formal tradition. And as Küng points out, it happened throughout the Protestant world,

> *And soon there was to be a Protestant 'orthodoxy' here, a new Protestant normative theology, which swore by the letter of the Bible and of Luther and which was often to be as intolerant of devIants and heretics as the Roman system.*[119]

A sectarianised Reformation in Ireland, Protestant and Catholic in opposition to each other, and colonial and political history hardened the traditions in opposition to each other. The closed systems became politicised and were not open to always being reformed. Faith was to be defended, not renewed. Whether the current diminishing practice of faith in Ireland is open to being shaken, judged, purged, and remade remains to be seen.

The Reformations were not just religious. Politics, economics, sociality and culture were all involved. Reform touched every dimension of the sixteenth century world. Reformed always to be reformed was as much political, economic, social and cultural as it was religious, and the challenge remains. All our institutions, of whatever kind, need always to be reformed. This is no less true in Europe today than it was when modern Europe was taking new shape in the sixteenth century. Does the European Union need reform? The Westminster Parliament, Dáil Éireann, the Northern Ireland Assembly? Of course they do otherwise they become moribund institutions, tired, ineffective and of no relevance to the people for whom they exist and to the pursuit of justice and peace, the heart of the common good which political and economic institutions are meant to serve. All need serious reform, not least the Northern Ireland Assembly and the way politics and democracy are practiced in Northern Ireland. But sometimes expecting those in power to bring about reform and change is like asking turkeys to vote for Christmas! But there is always the need for empowered and critical civil society to exercise people power and moral energy and the work of moral formation, that knows human limitations and temptations, and has critical awareness of a Protestant Principle and the need for on-going reform. When a society and its institutions become static it dies. There can be the tyranny not only of the past but of tradition, especially formalised tradition, closed off to reform and preventing the future.

There is a crisis of political, economic, cultural and religious legitimacy at present. With power and wealth moving from West to East, and the foreseeable future being Easternisation, and the end of a European and Western hegemon in world affairs and politics, there is growing fear and anxiety, which will easily be exploited by false messiahs of many kinds. Three political unions have dominated our lives for decades, the United States, United Kingdom and the European Union. It is not inconceivable that in the next two decades, each of these unions will begin to unravel. Reform will not be about renewing the status quo. It will need to be as radical and revolutionary as the Reformations of the sixteenth century, but with even greater necessity than then of being just and peaceful reform. Another bloody peasants revolt or thirty years war would be an even more unimaginable hell than the twentieth century.

Essential to any twenty-first century reform is robust and thorough moral reform, not some getting back to basics or a recovery of old landmarks, but radically new models of ethical values and praxis for a geopolitically changing twenty-first century world. Faith communities at their best have been communities of moral formation. If they want to be part of the reform movement, then they will need to engage more convincingly with public life, learn how to engage with the changing public square and how to apply social ethics to the great public and global questions of now. The sixteenth century Reformations were important, and by all means let's mark the 500th anniversaries. But we do not live in the sixteenth century. The world has changed and is changing again and we face different questions and different challenges. We need new political, social, economic and cultural models. And we need a new paradigm of theology and a new way of applying social ethics. The Christocentricity of the sixteenth century will become in the twenty-first century a human Christology and a peace Christology. Faith will recover the primacy of the human, which in relation to Jesus, will mean recovering the depth of his Jewishness, which was his humanness. Reform will recover the radically non-violent God of justice and peace and just peace and reconciliation will become the core practices and disciplines of the faith (faithful) community. Such reform will inform and shape an ethic of human and ecological flourishing, a robust social justice, gender justice, inter-religious justice and eco-justice ethic of life. Reformed always to be reformed.

References

1   Mortimer, Ian, *Centuries of Change: Which Century Saw The Most Change And Why It Matters To Us* (London: The Bodley Head, 2014) pp.130-131
2   Ibid, pp.129-130
3   Lindberg, Carter, *The European Reformations* (Oxford: Blackwell Publishers, 1996) pp.26-34
4   Mortimer, op.cit., p.126
5   Carter, op.cit., p.37
6   Ibid, p.37
7   Ibid, p.41
8   Ibid, p.41
9   Mortimer, op.cit., p.159
10 Eire, Carlos M. N., *Reformations: The Early Modern World, 1450-1650* (New Haven and London: Yale University Press, 2016) p.44
11 Ibid, p.51
12 MacCulloch, Diarmaid, *A History of Christianity: The First Three Thousand Years* (London: Allen Lane, 2009) p.571
13 Ibid, p.572
14 Eire, op.cit., p.41
15 Davies, Norman, *Europe: A History* (London: Pimlico, 1997) p.477
16 Eire, op.cit., p.65
17 MacCulloch, op.cit., p.595
18 Ibid, p.602
19 Davies, op.cit., p.478
20 Ibid, p.480
21 Eire, op.cit., p.68
22 Davies, op.cit., p.482
23 Ibid, p.484
24 MacCulloch, op.cit., p.609
25 MacCulloch, Diarmaid, *Reformation: Europe's House Divided* (London: Penguin Books, 2004) p.131
26 Davies, op.cit., p.485
27 Greengrass, Mark, *Christendom Destroyed: Europe 1517-1648* (London: Allen Lane, 2014) p.360
28 Ibid, p.362
29 Ibid, pp.363-364
30 Davies, op.cit., p.490
31 Greengrass, op.cit., 367
32 MacCulloch, *Reformation*, op. cit., p.xx
33 Ibid, p.172
34 Eire, op.cit., p.325
35 Ibid, p.327
36 Chadwick, Owen, *The Reformation* (London: Penguin-Books, 1990 edition) p.188
37 Ibid, p.188
38 Lindberg, op.cit., p.200
39 Ibid, p.202 The latter part of the quotation is from George Williams in his 1992 book *The Radical Reformation*.
40 Eire, op.cit., p.248
41 Ibid, p.250
42 Ibid, pp.260-261
43 Lindberg, op.cit., p.224
44 Ibid, p.225
45 Ibid, p.224
46 Eire, op.cit., p.276
47 Ibid, pp.369-371
48 Ibid, pp.371-372
49 Greengrass, op.cit., p.358
50 MacCulloch, *History of Christianity*, op.cit., p.657
51 Ibid, p.658
52 Duffy, Eamon, *Saints and Sinners: A History of the Popes* (New Haven and London: Yale University Press, 2006 Third Edition) p.203. The summary of Popes is from Duffy pp.196-225
53 Ibid, p.211
54 Ibid, p.212
55 Ibid, p.212
56 Ibid, p.214
57 Ibid, pp.214-215
58 Ibid, p.221
59 Eire, op.cit., p.378
60 Ibid, p.384
61 Karant-Nunn, Susan and Wiesner-Hanks, Merry E., *Luther on Women* (Cambridge: Cambridge University Press, 2003) p.197
62 Ibid, p.197
63 Watson, Natalie K., *Introducing Feminist Ecclesiology* (Sheffield: Sheffield Academic Press, 2002) p.28
64 Thompson, John Lee, *John Calvin and the Daughters of Sarah* (Genève: Librairie Droz S.A., 1992) p.4
65 Ibid, pp.7-8
66 Ibid, pp.9-10

67 Ibid, p.12
68 Eire, op.cit., p.712
69 Ibid, p.712
70 Ibid, p.714
71 Ibid, p.714
72 Ibid, p.717 Eire includes a portrait of Sister Jeronima, painted just before she left for Asia. She looks a very determined and self-confident woman.
73 MacCulloch, *A History of Christianity*, op.cit., p.670
74 Ibid, p.670-671
75 Elliott, Marianne, *When God Takes Sides: Religion and Identity in Ireland - Unfinished History* (Oxford: University Press, 2009) p.54
76 Tanner, Marcus, *Ireland's Holy Wars: The Struggle for a Nations Soul 1500-2000* (New Haven and London: Yale University Press, 2001) p.103
77 Bardon, Jonathan, *A History of Ireland in 250 Episodes* (Dublin: Gill and Macmillan, 2008) p.237
78 Elliott, op.cit., p.123
79 Ibid, p.124
80 Ibid, p.79
81 Eire, op.cit., p.526
82 Greengrass, op.cit., 394-395
83 Eire, op.cit., p.200
84 Ibid, p.201
85 Davies, op.cit., p.485
86 Eire, op.cit., p.206
87 Ibid, p.550
88 C. Veronica Wedgwood quoted in Davies, op.cit., p.563
89 Eire, op.cit., p.551
90 Davies, op.cit., p.565
91 Borman, Tracey, *Witches: James I and the English Witch Hunts* (London: Vintage Books, 2014) p.xv
92 Davies, op.cit., p.566
93 Borman, op.cit., p.xv
94 Greengrass, op.cit., p.395
95 Eire, op.cit., p.250
96 Ibid, p.204
97 Brown, Robert McAfee, *The Spirit of Protestantism* (Oxford: Oxford University Press, 1977) pp.214-215
98 See McKim, Donald K, *The Bible in Theology and Preaching: How Preachers Use Scripture* (Nashville: Abingdon Press, 1994) Other

models have been developed since 1994, including Queer Theology, and the increasing work on sexual orientation and hermeneutics or Biblical interpretation.
99 Gunter, W. Stephen et al, *Wesley and the Quadrilateral: Renewing the Conversation* (Nashville: Abingdon Press, 1997) p.38
100 Ibid, p.9
101 McMaster, Johnston in Spencer, Graham (Editor) *Forgiving and Remembering in Northern Ireland: Approaches To Conflict Resolution* (London: Continuum, 2011) p.131 *Chapter 7 On Fire with the Justice of God: Re-Reading Romans as a Political Proclamation Towards a Desired Future*, pp.129-147
102 Borg, Marcus J. and Crossan, Dominic, *The First Paul. Reclaiming the Radical Visionary Behind the Church's Conservative Icon* (London: SPCK, 2009) p.157
103 Jennings, Theodore W., *Outlaw Justice: The Messianic Politics of Paul* (Stanford: Stanford University Press, 2013) p.61
104 McMaster, op.cit., pp.146-147
105 Ozment, Steven, *Protestants: The Birth of a Revolution* (London: Fontana Press, 1992) p.217
106 Brown, op.cit., p.106 The story is adapted from Brown
107 Ozment, op.cit., pp.1-3
108 Eire, op.cit., p.518
109 Küng, Hans, *Christianity: The Religious Situation of Our Time* (London: SCM Press, 1995) p.584
110 Ibid, p.585
111 Ibid, p.542
112 Ibid, p.543
113 Quoted in Brown, op.cit., p.43
114 Daly, Gabriel, *The Church Always in Need of Reform* (Dublin: Dominican Publications, 2015) p.213
115 Quoted in Brown, op.cit., p.49
116 McNeill, John T., quoted in Brown, Ibid, p.45
117 McCarthy, Timothy G., *The Catholic Tradition: The Church in the Twentieth Century, 2nd Edition* (Chicago: Loyola Press, 1998) p.59
118 Ibid, p.66
119 Küng, op.cit., p.543